We have traversed a path that few have dared to.

We are continuing on a path that still fewer have the courage to follow.

We must pursue a path that even fewer can dream to pursue.

Yet, we must; we hold in trust the aims and aspirations of millions of our countrymen.

DR VERGHESE
KURIEN

The profits from the sale
of this book will be used to
honour deserving Class X and
XII students in India under the
Amul Vidyashree and
Amul Vidyabhushan Award
schemes.

First published in India in 2012 by Collins Business
An imprint of HarperCollins *Publishers* India
a joint venture with
The India Today Group

Copyright @ GCMMF 2012

ISBN: 978-93-5029-149-8

2 4 6 8 10 9 7 5 3

HarperCollins *Publishers*
A-53 Sector 57, NOIDA, Uttar Pradesh – 201301, India
77-85 Fulham Palace Road, London W6 8JB, United Kingdom
Hazelton Lanes, 55 Avenue Road, Suite 2900, Toronto, Ontario M5R 3L2
and 1995 Markham Road, Scarborough, Ontario MIB 5M8, Canada
25 Ryde Road, Pymble, Sydney, NSW 2073, Australia
31 View Road, Glenfield, Auckland 10, New Zealand
10 East 53rd Street, New York, NY 10022, USA

Printed and bound at
Thomson Press (India) Ltd.

Amul's India

Concept, design and co-ordination by DY Works

Based on 50 years of Amul advertising
by daCunha Communications

COLLINS BUSINESS
An imprint of HarperCollins Publishers

Acknowledgements

•••••

This book was created, conceptualized and designed by DY Works with contribution by daCunha Communications.

DY Works, India's largest and oldest brand strategy and design firm, has partnered Amul for almost a decade on brand rejuvenation and brand creation. The principal designer on the project was Deepa Kamath while Roop Gambhir was the project anchor.

DaCunha Communications, the original creators of the Amul campaign, curated and re-mastered the 250 hoardings that appear in the book. Their association with Amul has continued for almost five decades. Rahul daCunha personally sought out contributors such as Amitabh Bachchan and Shobhaa Dé and was deeply involved in the creation process.

Santosh Desai was integral to the early ideation and contributed the largest essay in the book, encompassing the Amul saga over the decades as a mirror of a changing India.

All the authors featured in the book contributed their writing or their thoughts without any commercial consideration.

Finally, a special thanks to R.S. Sodhi, who believed in the book and wholeheartedly supported it through its many phases.

Contributors:

ALPANA PARIDA

ALYQUE PADAMSEE

AMITABH BACHCHAN

ANIL KAPOOR

CYRUS BROACHA

HARSHA BHOGLE

MANISH JHAVERI

MILIND DEORA

RAHUL DACUNHA

RAHUL DRAVID

RAJDEEP SARDESAI

SANIA MIRZA

SANTOSH DESAI

SHOBHAA DÉ

SHYAM BENEGAL

SUNIL GAVASKAR

SYLVESTER DACUNHA

Contents

·····

• • • • •

Foreword

•••••

R.S. SODHI
Managing Director
Gujarat Co-operative Milk
Marketing Federation Ltd.
Anand, Gujarat.

Amul emerged as an offshoot of the Indian freedom movement, to give poor farmers the best returns for their milk by eliminating middlemen. Since then it has grown into a national brand that is respected and trusted in every corner of the country. The concept 'Taste of India', the Amul moppet, and the consistent advertising strategy have all contributed to the Amul success story.

A daily and essential food product has to provide the consumer with the confidence that it is not only tasty and nutritious, but that it is produced to the highest hygienic standards, and provided at a fair and acceptable price. This is the assurance that the Amul brand promises, and for over fifty years we have striven continuously to honour this commitment. We have renewed this by meeting, and often surpassing, the customer's expectations of quality, value for money, choice, availability and service.

This has been possible with the cooperation and combined efforts of a producer-owned and -controlled integrated system of production, procurement, processing and marketing.

Amul sponsored the Dutch cricket team and the Sauber Formula 1 racing team.

This book portrays how an endearing moppet and her tongue-in-cheek humour helped a milk producers' co-operative create a 'White Revolution'. It traces how Amul evolved as a brand by commenting on the popular political and social culture of India over the past four decades. Its topical, humorous and memorable hoardings continue to delight generations of Indians.

DaCunha Communications has been a longtime partner of Gujarat Co-operative Milk Marketing Federation (GCMMF) and is the creator of the Amul hoardings.

DY Works has partnered Amul over the years through brand creation and rejuvenation, and has conceived, designed and created this book.

The book goes beyond being an ordinary anthology to being a chronicle of India through the eyes of the Amul girl. The multiple contributions by prominent writers and thinkers add to its richness.

Amul will continue to participate in the development of the country by using all the profits from the sale of this book to honour deserving Class X and XII students in India under the Amul Vidyashree and Amul Vidyabhushan Award schemes.

Introduction

•••••

The Amul campaign tells the stories of India, a hoarding at a time. The hoardings are markers to the 'popular' history of India and have been followed by fans for decades. Seemingly ageless, this long-running campaign has captivated fans across all ages. I have been one such, for almost four decades now.

One cold afternoon in early 2010, I sat in the Amul boardroom with R.S. Sodhi, Kishorsinh Jhala and Jayen Mehta – the senior management team at Amul – telling them why, with our twin qualifications as Amul brand partners and fans of the most-loved brand in India, we felt it was necessary for Amul to do a book. Amul hoardings, created week after week by daCunha Associates, have captured the spirit of India with beguiling charm and no malevolence for nearly fifty years. We needed to celebrate these hoardings, which have been the most visible face of the brand for so many years, by making a book that would pay tribute to the 'Toast of a Nation.'

The most obvious thought was to put an anthology together, either sequentially – neatly classified by decades – or by subjects such as politics, Bollywood, sports, etc. Our quick audit of anthologies and their owners revealed characteristic behaviour – these were usually hardcover coffee-table books, expensive enough to be bought by the very few, and then put away, unread but brightly displayed on a prominent shelf. Very often, the unsold copies of these anthologies were highly visible on the discounted counters of bookstores and were picked up as 'gifts that are cheap but appear expensive'.

The cartoons or the columns that the anthology collates, work well when you see them appear one at a time, but when they appear all at once, they tend to get repetitive. The iconic Amul hoardings deserved better, and an anthology was not the answer. Given the popularity of the Amul girl, we wanted the book to be accessible to a larger audience and decided to do an affordable paperback instead of a coffee-table tome. As for the content, we wanted to create material that would be read, discussed, mulled over – rather than simply glossed over after the reader identified and chuckled over a few of his favourite hoardings.

The Amul hoardings meant different things to different people – furthermore, everyone seemed to have their favourites. It became obvious that we needed a book that captured many viewpoints. These would be vignettes creating a patchwork quilt of essays, snippets, selections and trivia – by prominent writers, celebrities and the subjects of the hoardings themselves.

Thus, we roped in Santosh Desai to write the main piece in the book – a commentary on how Amul hoardings, by picking out the most striking events of our times, became reflective of a changing India, and why they struck such a deep and enduring chord in an entertainment-starved India. Amitabh Bachchan, to our complete delight, had been collecting all the Amul hoardings that featured him and was happy to be interviewed as well as write for the book. We have his viewpoint on his personal experience and on the continuity of the campaign. The other 'subjects' were Rahul Dravid, Sunil Gavaskar, Sania Mirza and Milind Deora, and all of them graciously give us their viewpoints.

Equally of interest would be the Amul story itself and the early years of the campaign. Sylvester daCunha digs into his memory and archives to give us a revealing account of the genesis and evolution of the Amul girl. Rahul daCunha, who took over the baton over twenty years ago, has a series of observations and facts about the Amul campaign, while copywriter Manish Jhaveri takes us behind

AMUL HOARDINGS
HAVE CAPTURED
THE SPIRIT OF INDIA
WITH BEGUILING
CHARM AND
NO MALEVOLENCE
FOR NEARLY
FIFTY YEARS.

the scenes into what goes into an Amul ad, capturing the ideation and creation process, and then the process of the hoarding actually being put up.

It was a challenging task to identify different contributors who would have an interesting perspective and be willing to write a book for which there is no remuneration (the proceeds of this book will go to the Amul Vidyashree and Amul Vidyabhushan awards given to schoolchildren who have performed well in board exams), and most of all, have a strong point of view about the Amul hoardings.

Shobhaa Dé writes about women in the Amul hoardings, and her own theory about the role model for the Amul girl; Rajdeep Sardesai pens a poignant piece about what made Amul hoardings stand out in the Bombay of his youth; Harsha Bhogle, who gave me a long and arduous chase through his time in England and Australia and everywhere else, makes it all worthwhile with a brilliant piece on

IT WAS A CHALLENGING TASK TO IDENTIFY DIFFERENT CONTRIBUTORS WHO WOULD HAVE AN INTERESTING AND STRONG PERSPECTIVE...

THE BOOK IS
ESSENTIALLY
NON-LINEAR IN ITS
NARRATIVE.

the Amul brand and the cricket hoardings; Cyrus Broacha writes of his personal memories of the Amul billboards and Shyam Benegal on the making of *Manthan*, his feature film on the dairy co-operative movement; Alyque Padamsee speaks of the Amul girl as a brand icon while I do an analysis of the Amul brand.

The diverse viewpoints, topics and tonality have all contributed to this rich tapestry and the book is essentially non-linear in its narrative. You can read from anywhere and find it will captivate you, regardless.

ALPANA PARIDA
President, DY Works

The Amul story

•••••

Anand, once a dusty, serene farming village, is today a symbol of modern nationalism. What started in 1946 in a village in Gujarat as a small co-operative effort to bring economic freedom to farmers by releasing them from the clutches of self-serving middlemen, has developed into a movement that involves millions of farmers all over the country, and into an incredible ₹ 120 billion (US$ 2.4 billion) company!

Anand is today the headquarters of the Gujarat Co-operative Milk Marketing Federation Ltd (GCMMF) and brand Amul.

A small fledgling co-operative has developed into a phenomenal movement. Each day, milk is collected at village centres within easy reach of the farmer, thus easing the burden on him or her and ensuring that the milk is fresh. It is tested for quality and fat content on computerized equipment, making the process both fair and transparent. Cash payments are made based on the fat content of the milk, thus helping the farmer with his day-to-day requirements. A significant feature is that milk is purchased largely from women, thus economically and socially empowering them and giving them a measure of influence in decisions regarding their welfare and development.

8

AFTER INDEPENDENCE, DEDICATED LEADERS HERALDED A NEW DEMOCRATIC CONSCIOUSNESS.

After independence, dedicated leaders heralded a new democratic consciousness, and encouraged measures to accelerate the pace of progress. The foundation stone for their major dairy in Kaira was laid by Dr Rajendra Prasad, the first president of India, and it was inaugurated in 1955 by Pandit Jawaharlal Nehru.

When invited to commission the cattlefeed plant at Anand in 1964,

Prime Minister Lal Bahadur Shastri wished to spend one night at a farm, unaccompanied by anyone. Hesitantly, Dr Verghese Kurien, then general manager of Amul Dairy, took on this task. Shri Shastri and Dr Kurien sneaked out to a village where farmer Ramanbhai and his family welcomed their guest, unaware that he was the prime minister! Next morning, a relieved Dr Kurien met Shri Shastri, who had spent the night talking to farmers about their lives and problems, and their experiences with the co-operative movement. So impressed was he that he requested Dr Kurien to replicate this in the rest of the country. Thus was born the National Dairy Development Board, headquartered at Anand. For the first time, a national institution was located in an obscure village rather than in India's capital city.

The Amul Model

CONSUMER

❸
STATE CO-OP MILK MKTG FED

❷
DISTRICT MILK CO-OP UNION

❶
VILLAGE DAIRY CO-OP

MILK PRODUCER

// Establishes direct linkage between milk producers and consumers

// Eliminates middlemen

// Milk producers (farmers) control procurement, processing and marketing

// Professional management

ANAND IS
TRANSFORMED
INTO THE
MILK CAPITAL
OF INDIA.

Dedicated freedom fighters with integrity and a vision for the future, such as Tribhuvandas Patel, Sardar Vallabhbhai Patel and Morarji Desai, brought with them a realization that the true development of India must begin at the grassroots. They mobilized the collective strength of the farming community under the guidance of enthusiastic and devoted professionals like Dr Kurien and H.M. Dalaya, and well-wishers like Maniben (daughter of Vallabhbhai Patel), and forged relationships beyond the merely professional.

The primitive and basic rural working and living conditions encouraged a feeling of cooperation and caring amongst the largely city-bred professionals working together towards a common goal. Coming together in warm-hearted and selfless friendship were the Kuriens, the Variavas and Maniben, among others.

From the Milkman of India

●●●●●

Dr Verghese Kurien is the founder of the Gujarat Co-operative Milk Marketing Federation and the brain behind the development and success of the brand 'Amul'. He is known as the father of the 'White Revolution' in India and the architect of 'Operation Flood', which was the largest dairy development programme in the world.

Here, in a brief interview, he shares some of his thoughts on the popular and much-loved Amul campaign.

Q: Dr Kurien, this was a campaign that you initiated and gave your blessings to forty-six years ago and have supported through all the years. What are your thoughts…?

DR KURIEN: While the brand 'Amul' was registered in 1957, the advertising campaign started only in 1966–67. The Gujarat Co-operative Milk Marketing Federation, which markets the 'Amul' brand, came into being only about eight years later. Long before that, I realized that if we wanted to hold our own in the market, the professional services of an advertising agency were vital. My brother-in-law, K.M. Philip, very

I realize how wise a decision it was to give complete freedom to the ad agency to do their job in a professional way. I never interfered with their work and the result is before you. They have done an exemplary job.

13

astutely advised us to leave the business of advertising to the experts, and that's what we did. Looking back, I realize how wise a decision it was to give complete freedom to the ad agency to do their job in a professional way. I never interfered with their work and the result is before you. They have done an exemplary job.

Q: What do you feel the Amul girl has done for the brand?

DR KURIEN: The Amul girl has given the brand just the image we had in mind – that of a precious, 'priceless' product that the consumer could trust completely.

Q: Do you have any personal favourites among the hoardings?

DR KURIEN: It is difficult to choose one hoarding over the others; each one of them is on contemporary subjects close to the heart of the general public, and quite unique. They are also very witty, thought-provoking and humorous.

The 'Utterly butterly' story

•••••

SYLVESTER DACUNHA
is the chairman of
daCunha Communications.
In 1966, he co-created
the Amul butter hoarding
campaign, heralding the
birth of the longest-running
outdoor campaign of all time.

It was 1966. The advertising for a product called Amul butter was assigned to an agency of which I was the manager. The butter had been in the market for about ten years. It was positioned as, 'processed from the purest milk under the most hygienic conditions by a dairy co-operative in Gujarat'.

This was like a lantern lecture to an indifferent audience. Nonetheless, it had left some positive impressions about the brand. But clearly, some pep needed to be injected into the communication.

For a start, we needed a tag line to replace 'Purely the Best'. A new slogan dropped out of the sky when I told my wife Nisha about our new ad assignment. She spontaneously remarked, 'Why don't you say "Utterly Amul."' To which I added, 'Hey, what about, "Utterly butterly Amul!"' And so was coined a slogan that became one of the more memorable battle cries in advertising.

But the word 'butterly' initially met with some scepticism. 'It's ungrammatical,' objected a few. But Dr V. Kurien, the head of Amul, said, 'I think it's utterly mad; but if you think it'll work, go ahead.'

The Amul moppet today, against a backdrop of a hand-done strip dating from the early 1970s.

Our very first display presented the missy praying by her bedside.

A jockey holding a slice of buttered toast appeared during the horse-racing season.

The lassie and her line first appeared on a few lamppost boards in Mumbai. The public response was immediate: 'How cute!'

So there we had a very promising selling line. What we now needed was a spokesman to voice it. But who? Instinctively, I sensed it should be a child, someone impish and lovable. I explained this to my then art director, Eustace Fernandes, a brilliant visualizer and cartoonist. After a few tries he came up with this charming little poppet in a polka-dotted frock and a matching ribbon in her ponytail. She was licking her lips as though to say, 'Utterly butterly delicious.' Yes, she had all the qualities I was groping for – she was naughty, cuddly, innocent, smart; I knew we had a winner.

The lassie and her line first appeared on a few lamppost boards in Mumbai. The public response was immediate: 'How cute!'

So we decided to build an outdoor campaign around her. Hoardings as a medium are impactful if the locations are well chosen and the message compelling. Our very first display presented the missy praying by her bedside: 'Give us this day our daily bread – with Amul butter.' The feedback was very positive.

During the horse-racing season came 'Thoroughbread,' with a small jockey holding a slice of buttered toast. During the monsoons: 'Pitter-patter, pick-a, pack-a Amul butter.'

Calcutta in the 1960s was in the grip of hartals, with processions yelling 'Cholbe na!' ('Will not do!'). We turned that around to: 'Bread without Amul – cholbe na, cholbe na.' It drew a smile from many die-hard leftists.

The Hare Krishna movement was the target of an Amul jibe. 'Hare Rama, Hare Krishna – Hare Hare!' became: 'Hurry Amul, Hurry Butter – Hurry! Hurry!'

Slowly, we found we were exploiting situations which were current. But topical ads pose a challenge. They need to appear immediately after the issue breaks out; else they lose their immediacy. The news of 100 runs by a cricketing hero or the crowning of an Indian Miss World needed an immediate Amul response.

But the logistics of releasing an ad ordinarily took time – first identifying the topic, then creating the rough layout, presenting it to the client, incorporating the client's suggestions, often re-presenting it for the client's final approval; and only then making multiple artworks for distribution to hoarding contractors, who would then erect scaffolds for painters to climb up and do the needful. It could all take a week or more – much too long.

> Topical ads pose a challenge. They need to appear immediately after the issue breaks out; else they lose their immediacy.

Dr Kurien, an inspiring client, immediately saw the need to cut corners. He told us that we were free to operate without obtaining his okay. That was a rare gesture indeed, and it reflected his unique way of going about things – the same uniqueness that made him the father of the milk revolution.

Dr Kurien did, however, caution us not to step on people's toes, 'If you get into trouble because of your ads, be prepared to face the music by yourself.' But

This billboard was in protest
against the frequent hartals in
the Calcutta of the 1960s.

19

The Hare Krishna movement
was the target of an
Amul jibe.

Heralding the monsoons…

The controversial decision by London airport authorities on virginity tests on Indian women was the subject of the first billboard and elicited furious protests from women's rights groups, and so we extended a peace offering.

SYLVESTER
DACUNHA

Amul is probably the only campaign in the world with the theme and style unchanged in nearly fifty years.

when we did sometimes ruffle feathers, he stood by us. For instance, during a prolonged airline strike, a little uniformed air hostess said: 'Indian Airlines serves Amul butter – when it flies.' A furious airline demanded the immediate removal of the ad or threatened to stop serving Amul butter. Dr Kurien barked, 'The ad stays. No one's going to tell me how to run my advertising.'

There were a few other instances when our ads were controversial. The London airport authorities had taken a decision to conduct virginity tests on Indian women to verify their claims of having husbands already resident in the UK. We had spoofed: 'Indian virgin needs no urgin.' Protests were immediately heard from women's rights groups. We apologetically blanked the message to avoid offence to our sisters.

There have so far been over 4000 utterly-butterly hoardings. This is probably the only campaign in the world with the theme and style unchanged in nearly fifty years.

You might say that the ads represent a history of modern India acted out by a little heroine, healthy and confident about the future.

Amul's India

•••••

SANTOSH DESAI
is managing director of
Future Brands and one of
India's most original social
commentators. He regularly
writes a column, 'City City,
Bang Bang,' in *The Times
of India* on culture and
consumers. His book, *Mother
Pious Lady – Making Sense of
Everyday India*, is a critically-
acclaimed bestseller.

'It was Sharjah, boys, not Haar ja!' That is my
favourite, if not the most pleasant, memory of an
Amul hoarding. The occasion, of course, was India's
infamous loss to Pakistan, when Javed Miandad's
last-ball six dented not only the personal pride of the
individual spectator, but put a lingering question mark
in the national psyche about whether we had it in us
to face tough situations and come out on top. The
Amul hoarding captured our feeling perfectly, using
stiletto sarcasm instead of blunt criticism. Of course,
this was one of many Amul messages that came out
deliciously-timed and appropriately cheeky, and gave
us something to chuckle about. Growing up in an
entertainment-starved India, the opportunities for
amusement were few and needed to be contrived
through personal effort. In such a landscape, the
Amul billboard was a bracing shock of good cheer,
to be looked forward to and commented upon. Not
all messages elicited the same kind of reaction, but
somehow it was in the fitness of things that not
all Amul hoardings were blockbusters – that was a
reflection of how life unfolded.

With its combination of wry observation, heartfelt tribute, sly comment and the occasional controversial slip, the Amul billboard has watched over India.

1970s TO MID-1980s

Between the 1970s and the coming of economic reform in the mid-1980s, the Amul billboard documents the disconnected concerns of a small group. A surfeit of spectacularly trivial occasions are paid tribute to.

1985 TO MID-1990s

The Amul billboard covers the beginning of liberalization and the change in the political discourse.

POST 1991

The portrayal of the politician as villain begins to emerge with force at this time, with many references to a series of political scandals and controversies.

AFTER 2000

The movement towards the popular becomes increasingly pronounced as a very significant proportion of messages draws from Bollywood and television.

24

For nearly fifty years now, the Amul billboard has watched over India, punctuating its progress with wry observation, heartfelt tribute, sly comment and the occasional controversial slip. Its relationship with the country has been unique: unlike the newspaper, which offered a daily account of all important events, the Amul billboard was more selective, choosing the events it highlighted with more care. The considerations were many – the event had to be of sufficient interest, it needed to have some dramatic potential and, of course, there had to be a way of connecting with the brand, however superficial or contrived that link might be. The link with the brand was an important part of the charm of the message, for it gave some boundaries to the message and pushed the agency to greater creativity as a result of this constraint.

The nature of the Amul intervention was often very simple. In a lot of cases, it merely observed events and pointed them out. In a lot of billboards, there is little comment. The act of being a spectator, of merely marking out the moment and presenting it in a manner that caused us to smile, was often the only role it played. Of course, there were occasions when more pointed comment was felt to be in order, but overall, Amul used the platform it had in the national consciousness with restraint, something that has no doubt helped it stay relevant after so many years. By not overplaying its hand and being led away by its ability to frame debates, Amul avoided the corrosiveness that can come naturally to the habitual commentator. Tracing Amul's journey through the decades is in many ways akin to tracing India's journey, albeit through a specific and special vantage point.

Between the 1970s and the coming of economic reform in the mid-1980s,   25
the story of India as told through the Amul billboard is an interesting one. Not only
because of what it says but also because of what it does not. The Emergency is,
of course, referred to, and there are hoardings that refer to the mass sterilization
campaign, as well as the dreaded MISA (Maintenance of Internal Security Act).

A spoof on the mass sterilization diktat of Indira Gandhi's Emergency years, showing the unique
Amul ability to take a controversial subject and turn it into a joke.

26

Amul's delicious response to the world's first test tube baby in 1984.

A smart Amul salute to President Carter's 1978 visit.

Tennis player John McEnroe let his racket – and his mouth! – do the talking.

28   The other subjects and issues covered span a wide variety, including Jimmy Carter's 1978 visit ('We are peanuts about you'), Lata Mangeskhar's honorary doctorate (the elegant 'Doctor-ate' was the result), the first test tube baby ('Taste tube baby'), the first Jazz Yatra, the auction of the Nizam's jewellery, Gavaskar's double centuries, the Congress victories in 1981, the controversial virginity test (which elicited two hoardings – the risqué and insensitive 'Indian virgin needs no urgin,' followed by the contrite 'Urgin' our virgin – accept our peace offering'), McEnroe's on-court antics, Margaret Thatcher's election as Britain's first woman prime minister and the Congress (I)'s election campaign blitz in 1983.

The 1970s are usually regarded as the most difficult decade for the country as its founding ideals ran aground and found no competing vision to replace them. From the standpoint of the Amul hoarding, we catch only a fleeting glimpse of this reality. Perhaps the best index of the nature of these years comes in the number of hoardings that celebrate spectacularly minor events; it is tempting to think that as the national picture got gloomier, the hoardings sought out little islets of cheer and focused on them instead. For instance, in the period in question, we see hoardings about fashionable raincoats in Mumbai, a tribute to Chaplin's *Gold Rush*, a billboard about a vintage car rally, a tribute to an Indian becoming the head-boy at Eton (really), a strike by resident doctors and finally, one about an English girl marrying a Calcutta rickshaw-wallah (with the somewhat patronizing, if not bordering on offensive 'For butter or for worse').

1980 – Margaret Thatcher wins. Don't miss the somewhat laboured use of the word 'tory'.

The 1970s are usually regarded as the most difficult decade for the country… as the national picture got gloomier, the hoardings sought out little islets of cheer and focused on them instead.

The hoardings of this period also give us a sense of the schism that existed in the country between an India that lived in the metros, spoke and thought in English, and felt more at home with international developments than with what happened within the country. In this period the Amul hoardings are more literate and speak to the small microcosm represented by the educated liberal middle class. The choice of subjects is revealing – there is an enormous appetite for international subjects, and the allusions are redolent with inside references. That is not to say that the concerns of the ordinary Indian found no place in this landscape, but merely that a bulk of the messages were such that they would have made sense to a small group only. For this group, the Amul hoardings were highly evocative of the life they lived and the mental universe they inhabited.

The subjects covered in the mid-1980s indicate some interesting shifts.
The period between 1985 and 1990 is particularly instructive as the world went
through dramatic changes and the Amul billboards stood witness to these. We
see a discernible shift in the concerns addressed by Amul, as the focus on politics,
international affairs and aspects of economic reform took centre stage. The other
big change was the growing importance of popular culture, with many references
about cinema and television. The subjects covered included the end of the Cold
War, Tiananmen Square, Operation Desert Storm, the Bofors scandal, Ramayana
and Mahabharat on TV, the passing of Raj Kapoor, the introduction of the IPKF in

Operation Desert Storm in 1990 gets the Amul treatment.

32

When the Bofors scandal rocked the Rajiv Gandhi government.

Noting the Ramayana mania on TV.

Between 1985 and 1990, the world went through dramatic changes and the Amul billboards stood witness to these.

Sri Lanka, the Mandal Commission and the rise of V.P. Singh and, of course, the crowning achievement of them all – India's winning the kabbadi gold at the Asian Games.

33

We often think of liberalization as having been really ushered in in 1991, but in many ways, the most critical steps that helped bring about a change in the experienced reality of most Indians took place in the period between 1985 and 1991. The roots of the new political consciousness of the emerging classes and the beginning of a redefinition of the political power equation can be traced back to this time, as indeed can the development of the middle class as a consumer segment. This is also the time when the popular voice began to gain legitimacy and started to assume prominence in our consciousness.

The Amul take on the Mandal Commission.

34

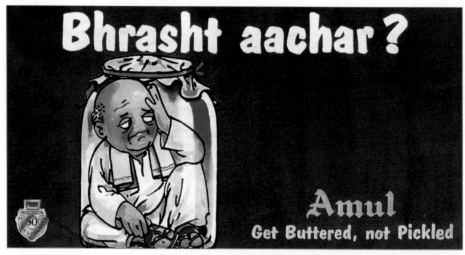

Delicious and very apt jibe at Narasimha Rao over his alleged involvement with a pickle baron.

Amul gives Jayalalitha some food for thought as she spends time in jail.

SANTOSH DESAI

POST
1991

Post 1991, popular culture becomes one of the primary modes through which change is experienced.

Post 1991, the twin forces of political empowerment of a new class as well as the assertive expansion of the world inhabited by the middle class can be seen clearly through the prism of Amul ads. The portrayal of the politician as villain begins to emerge with force at this time, with many references to a series of political scandals and controversies, namely, Jayalalitha going to prison, Kiran Bedi being shifted from Tihar, a billboard headlined 'Crookshastra', a play on Kurukshetra, referring to political murkiness in UP, Lalu Yadav's fodder scam, Narasimha Rao's alleged entanglement with a pickle baron (alluded to by the very clever 'Bhrasht-aachar'). The tone too becomes edgier and the hoardings show an increasing comfort with sharper barbs. One that stands out for its cheekiness is 'Party, Patni or Woh?', referring to the leadership tangle in the Congress involving Rao, Sonia Gandhi and V.P. Singh. It is during this period that popular culture becomes one of the primary modes through which change is experienced. The role of the media in framing our sense of reality becomes increasingly apparent. Hoardings marking the coming of satellite television, the advent of the third

The tone becomes edgier and the hoardings show an increasing comfort with sharper barbs.

36   umpire (a development hastened by the growing power of the television watcher), events like Miss Universe and Miss World, the controversy surrounding the advertising for Tuff shoes, all point to this new engagement with media.

References of business begin to creep in, with messages about the Open Sky policy that partially deregulated the aviation sector, the Enron Power controversy, the trouble faced by KFC in its first attempt to enter the country, a nod to Dr Manmohan Singh and his effort towards ushering in economic reform, an acknowledgement of the power of Maruti on the occasion of the launch of Zen, and a heartfelt tribute to J.R.D. Tata on the occasion of his passing, all highlight the growing importance of business and the world of consumption in the lives of the middle-class Indian.

The other notable change we see is in the involvement with the rest of the world, particularly the West. If, earlier, the ads were full of allusions to events in the West, in this period, we began to see good news travelling in the other direction as well. The interest in the West continued, with many ads that addressed this need, but events like Miss Universe and Miss World, Arundhati Roy's Booker win, the visit of Charles and Diana to the country, and the (somewhat questionable) achievement of having Yanni perform in front of the Taj, all marked a feeling that India's international profile was on the rise.

One of the more cheeky Amul hoardings referring to the leadership tangle involving Narasimha Rao, Sonia Gandhi and V.P. Singh.

A clever way to echo popular public sentiment: Kiran Bedi is ousted from Tihar.

38

The Tuff ad controversy – brought to us by Amul!

Cheeky, stark, simple – Amul on Enron in 1996.

Many allusions sit comfortably together in this hoarding on the launch of Zen by Maruti in the 1990s.

American fast food giant KFC had teething problems when it launched in India.

40

Yanni comes to the Taj Mahal – and Amul marks the event by remixing a popular ad.

Buttering up the saas-bahu: TV's staple for many years.

Nothing is too trivial for the Amul hoarding!

SANTOSH
DESAI

AFTER
2000

After 2000, we see both the amplification of existing trends in society as well   41
as the acknowledgement of some new forces. The movement towards the popular
becomes increasingly pronounced as a very significant proportion of messages
draw from Bollywood and television. Most major new film releases get their own
billboard and the overall drift towards celebrities and the titbitization of news finds
reflection in the tenor of the Amul campaign. We have hoardings referring to a
model's wardrobe malfunction in a fashion show as well as the controversy over
Katrina Kaif's skirt while on a visit to Ajmer Sharif. The importance of the symbolic
over the substantive finds expression in several messages; a sampling includes
Amitabh Bachchan's wax figure at Tussaud's, the visit of Brad Pitt and Angelina
Jolie to India as well as the controversies that surrounded it, the 'Pink Chaddi'

Two good: Angelina Jolie and Brad Pitt make a movie – and news – in Mumbai.

The engagement of the ads with the world of business and consumption continues to grow and… they start becoming active parts of our lived reality.

campaign, Aishwarya Rai's rumoured involvement in a Bond film, Shah Rukh Khan's brief detention at Newark airport, Ekta Kapoor's penchant for beginning her serials with the letter 'k', and Bipasha Basu's controversial kiss on the cheek to Cristiano Ronaldo.

The engagement of the ads with the world of business and consumption continues to grow and we can see how they start becoming very active parts of our lived reality. The UTI scandal, tributes to popular advertising campaigns like Coke's 'Thanda Matlab Coca Cola' and Vodafone's Zoo-Zoos, a comment on the volatile Sensex ('Nonsensex?'), the introduction of the revolutionary Tata Nano as well as the problems it faced in West Bengal, the new VAT proposals, the investment in DreamWorks by Anil Ambani and the war between the Ambani brothers, all feature in the Amul campaign. We also begin to see references to the disquiet caused by rapid liberalization. The impact of flyovers, the proposal to build a mall in front of the Taj Mahal ('Taj Mall?'), the 2G scandal, the Satyam scandal ('Satyam, Sharam, Scandalam!'), all begin to find a mention, in keeping with the national mood.

To protest against the attack on women in a Mangalore pub, an Internet-based group launched a drive to send pink underwear to the head of the moral police brigade.

Bollywood references multiply the Amul way: actress Bipasha Basu and footballer Cristiano Ronaldo lip synch!

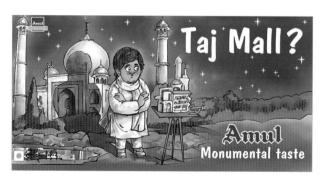

Uttar Pradesh chief minister Mayawati's ill-conceived shopping mall near the Taj Mahal gets a taste of Amul.

44

Too obvious to miss: The introduction of Value Added Tax (VAT) wasn't received well!

One word that summarized our feelings about the stock market.

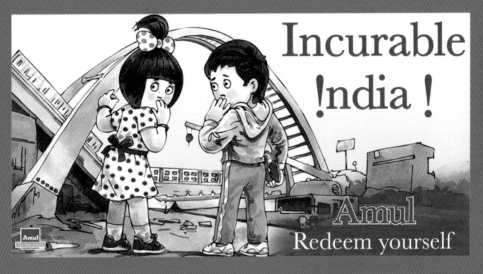

Disgust – the Amul way: A parody on the line 'Incredible India', this hoarding referred to the Commonwealth Games scam in New Delhi.

It is striking that among the several obituary hoardings that were put up during this period, not even one lamented the passing of a political leader.

46

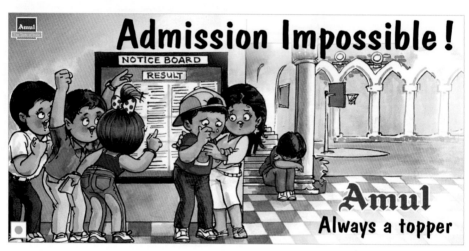

Everyday concerns such as school and college admissions became part of the Amul campaign.

The anger against the political class continued to become sharper and the hoardings in this period seldom pulled punches when it came to political scandals. 'No Koda of conduct' (Madhu Koda's alleged Rs 400-crore scam in Jharkhand), 'Maya ne khaya?' (the court case against Mayawati), 'Beta ban gaya neta' (the tendency of politicians' progeny to carry on the family business), 'Incurable India' (the great CWG bungle), all displayed a streak of undisguised disgust with the ruling class. We find relatively fewer positive messages about the leaders of the country; it is striking that among the several obituary hoardings that were put up during this period, not even one lamented the passing of a political leader. We had tributes to film actors and directors (Ashok Kumar, Mehmood, Johnny Walker, Hrishikesh Mukherjee, Amrish Puri), artists, writers and musicians (Michael Jackson,

The politician plunges further in public estimation: Detecting an alleged scam by Jharkhand chief minister Madhu Koda, involving mining contracts.

George Harrison, M.F. Husain, Bombay's own Busybee, Bhimsen Joshi) and people like Dilip Sardesai and Sam Manekshaw, the choice clearly indicating the kind of people that enjoy popular respect and appeal in Amul's India.

Along with greater disenchantment with the political class has come a deeper engagement with the problems of everyday life. The Amul hoarding has started becoming part of the citizen-journalist discourse, as the middle class seeks to develop a voice and make its presence felt in the larger scheme of things. The slow decline in the political significance of this class, arising out of the changes that were brought into effect in the previous decade, coupled with the growing power of public-media platforms, has meant that the space occupied by the

Billboards like 'Eeek-mail' (documenting a deadly virus), 'i-Fun' (the popularity of the i-Phone) and 'Facebhook?' (the rise of Facebook), all recognized the new role of the Internet in our lives.

48

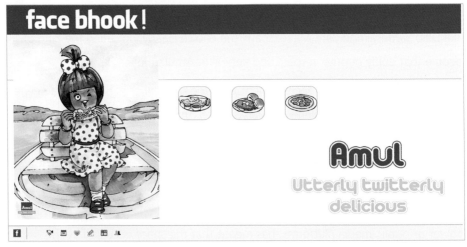

Amul campaign plays an additional role of communicating the grievances of its

49

consumers as they go about the business of their everyday lives. Power shortages, bad roads, the impossibility of getting college admissions, even the raising of the legal age for drinking, all become material for the campaign.

The other significant change seen during this period is, of course, the importance of the Internet and the many changes this has brought about. Billboards like 'Eeek-mail?' (documenting a destructive virus), 'Dotty about coms' (the dotcom explosion), 'Face-bhook!' (the rise of Facebook), 'i-fun' (the popularity of the i-phone), all recognize the role being played by this new medium in our lives. We also notice the first references to issues of alternative sexuality, with a message like 'Out of the closet, out of the fridge' marking the Delhi High Court judgement legalizing homosexuality.

50

'Out of the closet, out of the fridge!' – Amul's references to issues of alternative sexuality.

Referring to the Delhi High Court's landmark judgement, legalizing homosexuality.

... the growing disease called terrorism.

Amul was quite vocal in its response to the inertia of our politicians post the 26/11 terror attacks.

Echoing the public anger against the long-drawn-out trial of Ajmal Kasab.

This was a call to all Mumbaikars to rise up and act, post the 2011 bomb blasts.

Perhaps the biggest change, both in terms of content and tone, lay in the   53
treatment of the growing disease called terrorism. It is striking how the campaign
tenor changes when addressing this subject; examples include 'Will the real
terrorists please stand up', showing a politician being guarded by security, a verse
from the song 'Seene me jalan, ankhon mein toofan' and 'Bas ab aur nahin, Kasab
aur nahin,' documenting the anger against the long-running trial of Kasab. When
it comes to terrorism, the campaign loses its ability to allude to current events, no
matter how disturbing, with a lightness of touch. Its tone is in keeping with the
larger reaction this subject evokes and is reflective of the times we live in.

The billboards... have become a kind of moving
timeline marking what we have considered
significant at various points of time in our past.

Overall, the Amul campaign is a very interesting vantage point from which
to see the history of our lived experiences, particularly if we come from urban
middle-class India. The billboards have, through the choice of their subjects, the
breezy manner in which they are brought to our attention, and by the very act
of staying current, become a kind of moving timeline marking what we have
considered significant at various points of time in our past. The great advantage of
the Amul campaign is that it has never tried too hard to make a comment; it is by
highlighting a subject with gentle humour and unerring timing that it allows us to
think about the event, using our own perspective.

54

The river that is India flows on, and the brand that is Amul continues to give us a running commentary on what it sees, feels and experiences...

The story of Amul's India is also one of a country coming in touch with itself, even as it transforms beyond recognition. From a somewhat disconnected class living in a world of its own, we see a country create its own narrative, with its own distinctive language, its own set of heroes, its own set of issues, and do battle with its weaknesses. The river that is India flows on, and the brand that is Amul continues to give us a running commentary on what it sees, feels and experiences as it accompanies us on this glorious ride.

What makes the Big B smile

•••••

AMITABH BACHCHAN

Amitabh Bachchan is without a doubt our greatest screen icon and idol.

Over the years, the Big B has been a favourite for writer Manish Jhaveri and myself – whether it's been his wax double at Madame Tussauds, his down-to-earth warmth on *Kaun Banega Crorepati*, or his colourful array of celluloid characters, the two of us truly enjoy doing Amul hoardings on the superstar – and our wonderful artist Jayant Rane caricatures him with a unique relish.

So when a book was planned on the history of this campaign, we knew it would never be complete without talking to this matinee magician. I was particularly keen to ask the great man if the billboards meant something to him personally. I met him at his tastefully decorated office, in a quiet bylane of Juhu.

– Rahul daCunha

RD: What exactly does the campaign signify to you personally and to the film industry in general?

AB: I think it is a unique marketing device. Giving the brand a caricature, an emblem, a finite identity and then bringing it across with humour, satire and sarcasm to reflect current affairs, has been most

The song 'Khaike paan Banaraswalla' from the 1978 Amitabh movie, *Don*, had everyone from taxi drivers to tiffinwallahs singing.

58

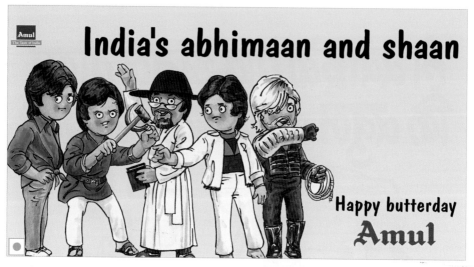

Amul wished the great man on his birthday, using two of his immortal films – *Shaan* and *Abhimaan*.

innovative. It is a departure from the straight in-your-face pronouncement of the product. It therefore has a threefold effect as opposed to perhaps one in all the others – the brand, the humour and the topicality. For the film industry and for the films that get mention in the campaign, it's free publicity; a boon for all producers struggling to maximize on awareness without spending. And yes, it does reflect and become a yardstick for success. I cannot say for the others, but when the campaign covers a film of mine, I take it as an endorsement by the public of its success. It goes the same way for failure too.

RD: Is it true that you keep a copy of the posters where you are featured?
AB: Yes, indeed, I do!

59

A tribute to the lost-and-found formula hit *Amar Akbar Anthony*, starring Bachchan, Vinod Khanna and Rishi Kapoor.

RD: Where do you feel that the Amul campaign fits into the modern world of twitter and 'trending'... does it need to adapt to modern technology?

AB: If it ain't broke, don't fix it!! Leave the campaign as it is. Change does not always prove successful. The great American icon, John Wayne, never got off his horse in any of his films!

The campaign has become, quite inadvertently, the equivalent of 'trending' on social networking sites. It has adjusted itself, without any effort, to the modern world. Great poetry, like great wine, is measured by the number of years it lasts, without change!

The 1991 mega movie, *Hum,* had the hit number 'Jumma chumma de de.'

Bachchan switched roles to TV show host with amazing ease on the quiz programme, *Kaun Banega Crorepati*.

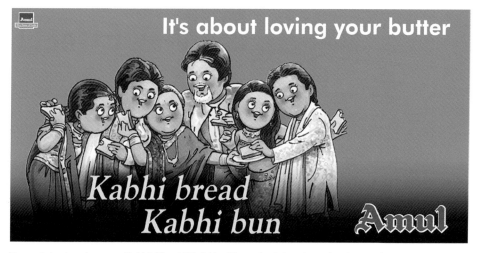

Karan Johar's epic saga, *Kabhi Khushi Kabhie Gham*, had the Big B dancing and emoting with equal élan.

The Big B-starrer, *Paa*, became Khaa!

Madame Tussauds paid homage to the legendary actor.

The campaign has become… the equivalent
of 'trending' on social networking sites.

Amul tweeted the Big B a speedy recovery.

Starstruck Amul

·····

BOLLYWOOD

… most of its popular stars have been widely featured in the Amul hoardings over the years.

SALMAN KHAN
VIDYA BALAN
AAMIR KHAN
SHAH RUKH KHAN
HRITHIK ROSHAN
SANJAY DUTT
ABHI-ASH

Salman Khan

Sallu, as he is popularly known, is Bollywood's most controversial Khan – his flying fists are as talked about as his flying kisses. His popularity can be judged by both his housefuls and the queues outside his Bandra house. He is the industry's most realiably saleable star, with mega hits like *Dabangg* and *Bodyguard*.

The brawny star's *Biwi No 1* was the biggest blockbuster of 1999.

The actor's constant brush with the law has always made headlines.

Salman is also a very friendly, successful TV presenter.

The pun was a spoof on the item song, 'Munni badnaam hui, darling tere liye,' from the superstar's hit film, *Dabangg*.

Vidya Balan

While all modern-day heroines strive for the size-zero body, Vidya has never shied away from flaunting her voluptuous curves. And while other actresses have to settle for hero-oriented films, Balan's heroine-dominated *The Dirty Picture*, based on the life of sex siren Silk Smitha, won her accolades and statuettes.

This hoarding parodied the hit song, 'Ibn-e-batuta,' from Vidya's popular film, *Ishqiya*.

Vidya's role of sex siren Silk Smitha in the 2011 movie, *The Dirty Picture*, made her a national icon.

Aamir Khan

He is the quietest of the Khans, but everything he touches invariably turns to silver, gold and diamond jubilees. From *Qayamat Se Qayamat Tak* to *Rang De Basanti* and from *Delhi Belly* to *3 Idiots*, this man has always had his finger on India's pulse.

Aamir's cricket saga, *Lagaan*, was a true Bollywood landmark.

The catchy number, 'Aati kya Khandala,' from the 1998 Aamir starrer, *Ghulam*, had India humming.

His 2006 film, *Rang de Basanti*, defined an entire generation and gave the youth an identity.

Aamir and Kiran Rao had a baby through IVF surrogacy. (The headline plays on a song from the actor's early hit, *Qayamat Se Qayamat Tak*.)

SRK played a dashing fighting machine in *Don* and *Don 2*.

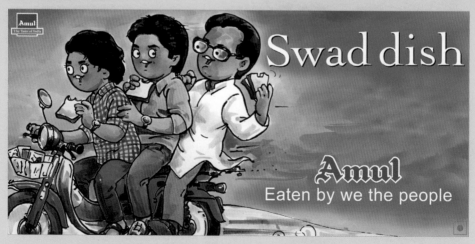

The movie *Swades* was a pun waiting to happen.

Shah Rukh Khan

SRK is one of our greatest-ever screen icons. No mean feat for a long-haired lad who came from Delhi in the 1980s seeking fame and some fortune. This man has climbed very mountain there is, and achieved every success from KKK (The Kolkata Knight Riders) to *K-K-K-Kiran*, his award-winning performance in *Darr*. He is truly Shahrukh.One.

74

After SRK allegedly slapped film-maker Shirish Kunder at a film party.

The Karan Johar-directed *My Name Is Khan* inspired this billboard.

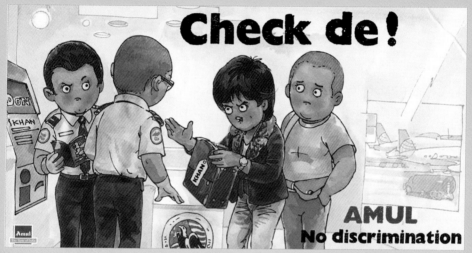

Shah Rukh was stopped at a US airport and detained for questioning (the headline was a pun on his jubilee hit, *Chak De India*).

The cine star's superpower film, *Ra.One*, easily morphed into 'Kha.One.'

Hrithik Roshan

This green-eyed heart-throb is the blue-eyed boy of the masses. He can dance, he can dazzle, he can *Dhoom*, and he can *dhamaka*. From *Kaho Na… Pyaar Hai* to *Koi Mil Gaya*, not to mention *Kites*, this Roshan is a trailblazer.

The green-eyed youngster burst onto the Bollywood scene with a hit in his very first foray, *Kaho Na… Pyaar Hai.*

'Frresh' was a take-off on Roshan's role as superhero, *Krrish*.

The 2010 Hrithik-starrer *Kites* flopped but this hoarding was a hit!

Sanjay Dutt

Sanju Baba deserves a chapter of his own when the ultimate Bollywood tome is finally written. His personal life has always been as newsworthy as his persona on screen. But what has always held him in good stead is his charm and charisma. Sanjay Dutt is truly everyone's 'Munnabhai.'

Sanjay Dutt was suspected of having links with terrorists (the headline refers to his 1999 film, *Vaastav*).

The Munnabhai series of films became a modern-day cult.

Sanju baba pleaded his own innocence, via a song from his 1993 film, *Khalnayak*.

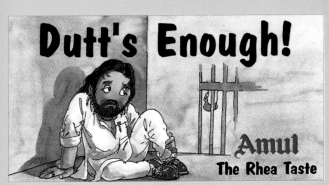

This hoarding referred to the injustice of Dutt's extended jail sentence.

Abhi-Ash

Abhishek Bachchan and Aishwarya Rai are one of Bollywood's most glamorous couples. Their personal lives have pretty much made them our desi Brangelina! Not for nothing are they jointly referred to as Abhi-Ash...

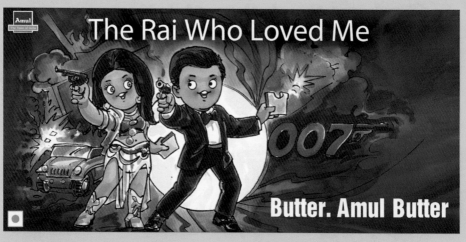

Aishwarya Rai almost became a Bond girl.

Amul parodied the 2005 Abhi-Rani starrer, *Bunty Aur Babli*.

The Bollywood thriller, *Dhoom 2*, was perfect to spoof.

Abhishek played a conman in the movie *Bluffmaster*.

Abhishek and Aishwarya's marriage ceremony was conducted between the two Bachchan homes – Prateeksha and Jalsa.

India waited with bated breath for the first Abhi-Ash baby.

The phenomenon of stars endorsing brands has also been the subject of many Amul hoardings.

Shah Rukh advertised Lux soap.

Aamir played a variety of interesting local characters in a popular Coke campaign.

At one time, all the three Khans of Bollywood were endorsing the three leading fizzy brands.

Iconic figures, real or imagined, evolve over time

●●●●●

SHOBHAA DÉ

Bestselling novelist, freelance writer and columnist, Shobhaa is well known for her frank and forthright comments on social and political issues.

Author photograph: Gautam Rajadhyaksha

It starts with the short skirt. The polka dots. And, of course, an attitude to match. It was always there! From the word 'go'. The cheeky little Amul girl pranced into our hearts in 1966, with her impish appeal and deceptive innocence. It is safe to state that she was really one of India's pioneering feminists… and I have my own theory about how that may have come about. Icons can never be created out of nothingness. Nor can they be constructed cold-bloodedly. Not even the smartest copywriter can claim that he or she decided one fine day to give birth to an 'icon' for a brand… and then succeeded in the mission. If only it was that easy! Iconic figures, real or imagined, evolve over time. Whether it's Mickey Mouse or Anna Hazare. And yes, it's quite okay to speak of them (Mickey and Anna) in the same breath. Icons forge a visceral connect with followers. It is a deeply emotional bond that stands the test of time.

That's what happened with the Amul characters – they managed to wriggle their way into our lives in a way that was entirely charming, non-intrusive and lovable. This could not have been strategically planned – of that, I am certain. But the girl's persona was no happy

But the girl's persona was no happy accident, I'm equally certain! Why? Don't ask. It's a girl thing...

The Amul girl... was always direct but never strident.

accident, I'm equally certain! Why? Don't ask. It's a girl thing… a gut feeling that defies deconstruction… challenges logic.

Here's my theory: The Amul campaign has been a family business from day one. It has remained the sole property of the talented daCunha family. Those timely and consistently lively billboards have long been attributed to the combined genius of the daCunha brains – *pere et fils*. Sylvester and Rahul. No doubt, with valuable inputs from other copywriters belonging to their stable. But it is widely acknowledged that the enduring Amul ads emerged from what is essentially a mom-and-pop show. Aha – now, here comes my googly. While the 'pop' in this case can stake his legitimate claim as the grandfather of the Amul family, what's the bet the girl was the 'mom's' brainchild? Huh? Puzzled?

The 'mom' I'm talking about is the hugely gifted writer, Nisha daCunha. I was privileged enough to be her student at St Xavier's College in Mumbai, and my love for literature and words can be directly traced to those inspired and inspirational lectures Nisha conducted with such supreme elegance and eloquence. Fiery, articulate, erudite and yet, so like a delicate flower, Nisha's views were passionate and fierce… so ahead of the curve. So appealing to anybody lucky enough to have her share them. I'm pretty sure it was Nisha who influenced the personality of the Amul girl, who breathed life into her representation. And who contributed to some of those on-the-button comments about women and their position in Indian society. The Amul girl, like Nisha, was always direct but never strident. Whether she was taking a stand on Mayawati or Jayalalitha, the 'voice' was consistently pro-women.

Feminist scholars may discover all kinds of messages in the lively series of hoardings that tracked milestone events depicting the rapidly changing status of women.

FIERY, ARTICULATE, ERUDITE AND YET, SO LIKE A DELICATE FLOWER, NISHA'S VIEWS WERE PASSIONATE AND FIERCE... SO AHEAD OF THE CURVE.

NISHA DACUNHA

The Amul girl became a spokesperson in a way
... acknowledging contributions, both national and
international, celebrating female achievements…

90

Amul has followed the
political fortunes of the
Uttar Pradesh leader,
Mayawati, with
great interest.

Tamil Nadu's iron lady,
Jayalalitha, is another
Amul favourite.

Celebrating Arundhati Roy's Booker Prize, the first for an Indian woman writing in English.

This may have happened unconsciously, minus an artificial construct. But it happened! And that's the remarkable part. Feminist scholars may discover all kinds of messages in the lively series of hoardings that tracked milestone events depicting the rapidly changing status of women. Whether those billboards featured game-changers like Arundhati Roy and Rakhee Sawant or hardcore politicians like Hillary Clinton and Benazir Bhutto, any woman who made it to the ubiquitous Amul hoarding was saying something powerful about being female. The Amul girl became a spokesperson in a way, commenting on policies influencing the collective destinies of women… acknowledging contributions, both national and international, celebrating female achievements… or merely chuckling over the foolishness of men.

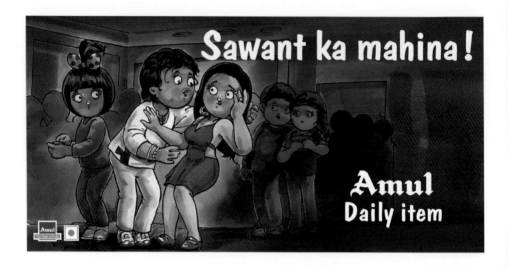

Whether those billboards featured game-changers like Arundhati Roy and Rakhee Sawant or hardcore politicians like Hillary Clinton and Benazir Bhutto, any woman who made it to the ubiquitous Amul hoarding was saying something powerful about being female.

Men have always tried to be chauvinists in Parliament – not always successfully.

All this was done subliminally, subtly… as points were made and popular
opinion reflected through clever copy that nudged viewers to think out-of-the-box,
adopting a tone that was conspiratorial, light-hearted, playful and non-preachy.

95

Over time, the Amul girl became 'our girl'… we join her as she pays a unique
tribute, not just to the absolutely terrific women of India and the world, but to one
specific woman who started it all.

Take a bow, Nisha!

Amul celebrates
India's great success in
international beauty
pageants.

Medha Patkar has won
Amul's admiration for
her resolve regarding the
Narmada Dam Project.

I can't remember a day without the Amul hoarding

•••••

CYRUS BROACHA
Stand-up comedian, political satirist, theatre and TV personality and columnist – some of the many faces of the inimitable Cyrus Broacha.

Generally, foreign tourists in Mumbai are given four locations as a must-see – the Gateway of India, Film City, Chowpatty beach, and above all, the Amul butter hoarding! Quite frankly, I can't remember a day without the Amul hoarding. Mind you, often, when times were tough, I remember plenty of days without butter itself. But not a single day without the Amul butter hoarding. However, looking at it and being part of it are two different things.

Since the story leading me to work on the hoarding would take roughly 785 pages, let me start right away. Okay you're right, no point. Let's fast forward to me working as a trainee copywriter at daCunha Associates, which handled the Amul butter account. The agency was run by the iconic and eccentric Sylvester daCunha and his son, Rahul. I worked under a military strategist called Kunal Vijayakar, copywriter, which in those days meant you worked roughly seven minutes per week.

Fortunately for me, I occasionally got to dedicate my seven minutes to the Amul butter hoardings. There were two that I loved the best. The first

There were two that I loved the best. The first…
coincided with the dismantling of apartheid
and Nelson Mandela's long walk to freedom.

"Lara, kya mara!"

Amul BUTTER

The line became extremely popular... whenever Lara scored heavily, Indian papers and the electronic media played the old refrain '*Lara, Kya Mara*!'

was, 'One man, one vote, one butter,' which coincided with the dismantling of apartheid in South Africa and Nelson Mandela's long walk to freedom. It would have been great if we could have sent the great man a copy of the hoarding along with a case of butter. But Sylvie ran a tight ship, and import and export was not encouraged at that point!

The other one that became popular was all thanks to a fruit platter. The fruit platter (still available at Nariman Point) is where all the local philosophers and poets meet, often times disguised as taxi drivers and underworld copywriters. Now, in the early part of 1994, Brian Charles Lara broke cricket's greatest record – Gary Sobers' 365 not out. We needed to encapsulate this in a hoarding.

Being a cricket fanatic, I was prepared to write reams and reams of print. Brevity, of course, was the challenge. Then I heard it... a modern-day Socrates with a thick, Maharashtrian accent said the immortal words, 'Lara, Kya Mara.' In true advertising tradition we ripped the poor guy off and covered ourselves with glory. The line became extremely popular and in the next few years of his career, whenever Lara scored heavily, Indian papers and the electronic media played the old refrain, Lara, Kya Mara!

Not just these, there are so many more examples. How a small hoarding in south Mumbai could have such long-lasting and wide impact is far beyond the capacity of this writer, to explain. Suffice it to say that each and every citizen of our city would easily have some tale or association with this uniquely awesome institution. At the risk of sounding a little right-wing – Amul hoarding ki jai!

SCAMS

The Indian ethos has always been to 'get rich quick'. An endearing quality when it works within the ambit of the law. Not so when public money is at stake – just 2011 alone witnessed countless scams: 2G, the Radia tapes, spot fixing, Adarsh Society, CWG, the list is endless. While there have been many serious scandals over the decades, Amul always managed to see the light-hearted side to them.

Former Union minister Sukh Ram was implicated in the 1993 telecom scam case.

This spot is fixed for Amul butter

Spot fixing is the new scam in cricket!

The Big Payoff

Amul

This 1976 classic was Amul's earliest comment on political scams.

Indian stockbroker Harshad Mehta earned the nickname 'Big Bull,' because he started the bull run.

The 2G telecom scam could well be India's largest scam ever, implicating several ministers too.

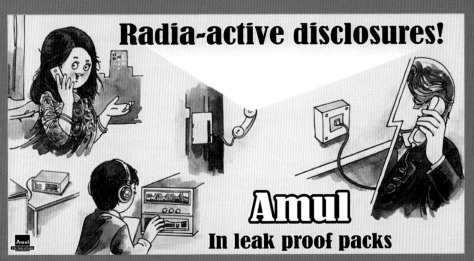

The Radia tapes controversy relates to telephonic conversations between political lobbyist Nira Radia and influential people, including the then telecom minister, A. Raja.

Suresh Kalmadi had to spend time in jail for his role in the Commonwealth Games scandal.

" It was a tremendous feeling... to find myself on an Amul hoarding

104

SANIA MIRZA

Sania is the first Indian woman to be listed in the top 30 WTA rankings. She has been honoured with the Arjuna Award and the Padma Shri for her outstanding accomplishments in the field of tennis.

Amul is a brand that everyone is so familiar with. Its products, whether butter, cheese, milk or ice cream, are always on the table. But the Amul hoardings and the antics of the Amul girl are a reminder of the brand even as one is passing by. I always enjoy seeing them as they are always relevant and play on current events.

As a tennis player and someone who is interested in all sports, I have noticed that the achievements of leading sporting greats in all fields have been acknowledged in such a timely and interesting way on the Amul hoardings. So, it was a great pleasure and surprise to see myself featured with the catchy phrase 'You are my Sania.' The hoardings have featured tennis stars such as Andre Agassi, Steffi Graf, Pat Cash and Roger Federer, to name only a few, so it was a tremendous feeling to find myself also on an Amul hoarding like these great players. It also gave me the feeling that the people were so proud of me and thus my achievements were not just for myself but for the entire nation.

To be on the same platform with so many eminent personalities who have been featured on the Amul hoardings has felt great.

When I got married two years ago there was so much media interest, particularly as my husband is also a popular Pakistani cricketer. I loved the hoarding done on us by Amul with a play on both our names! It was so clever and we were both very amused, and particularly delighted with the 'Indo-Pack' association!

Amul doffed its hat to Roger Federer's amazing tennis skills.

Andre Agassi had a penchant for the wildest, wackiest hairstyles in his playing days.

I loved the hoarding done on my husband and me with a play on both our names!

Satire is a double-edged sword in India

•••••

RAHUL DACUNHA

Rahul daCunha is managing director and creative head of daCunha Communications, the ad agency that creates the Amul outdoor billboards. He co-wrote the award-winning *Hamara Bajaj* campaign, and won a Gold from the Art Directors Club (New York) for his creative work on Shopper's Stop. Rahul has also written/directed plays like *I'm Not Bajirao*, *Pune Highway* and *Class of '84*.

I worked on my first Amul hoarding in June 1993. Nineteen years and 1500 hoardings later, I never tire of spoofing India. Here are a few things that fascinate me about this campaign:

- A little cartoon girl with blue hair and a red-and-white polka-dotted dress continues to be so relevant and revered even after nearly fifty years. It's like she's the daughter of the nation (One time, I frivolously put her in a mini skirt, in a hoarding that spoofed the IPL cheerleaders. The feedback was not good!)

- Every single Monday morning, it is decision time for me and my creative team – what current event do we spoof? What issue is India annoyed about or amused by? The daily papers throw up scams, scandals, soap operas, the share bazaar, Sachin, Shah Rukh – all grist for the Amul mill. Or should we tackle Amitabh's new film, Anna's new demand, America's new move, Amar Singh's new scandal, Ashton's new twitter? Very rarely is there a pan-India subject – that's how diverse and disparate the nation is. The south doesn't really

… every single Monday morning, it is decision time for me and my creative team – what current event do we spoof?

In the 1990s we didn't think twice about spoofing politicians – in this case a parody on chief minister Lalu Prasad Yadav's alleged involvement in the Rs 950-crore Bihar fodder scam.

speak Hindi. The east doesn't really watch Bollywood. Most of India is clueless about what happens in Bombay. And the Hindi belt is obsessed with local politics. So the Amul creative team often creates region-specific hoardings.

- By and large, the nation enjoys hoardings created in Hindi, so long as the language is simple, preferably Bollywoodized.

- We now live in a world with diminishing attention spans – news becomes old hat very quickly. Back in the 1980s, a topic could last upto a fortnight – now, we change hoardings every three days.

- As recently as the 1990s, we lived in more accepting, accommodating times. Take a hoarding we put up in Patna, lampooning Lalu Prasad Yadav as the

Light-heartedness has often led us to the doorstep of the legal process.

The then BCCI president, Jagmohan Dalmiya, wasn't pleased with this questioning of his integrity.

Amul gets scathing about the politically connected godman, Chandraswami.

We received a typed letter from Satyam's board objecting to our billboard, demanding we apologize... or their employees will stop using Amul products!

'Fodder of the nation', signing off with 'Scamul' – totally unmindful of the consequences. Or when we scathingly called godman Swami Chandraswami, 'Chandraslimy?' Today, try poking fun at the MNS in Mumbai or satirizing Mayawati in Meerut. Sure we have freedom of expression compared to, say China, but we're a democracy only in principle.

- Light-heartedness has often led us to the doorstep of the legal process. In 2000, Jagmohan Dalmiya, erstwhile BCCI chief, attempted to sue Amul for 500 crores because we ran a hoarding asking the probing question, 'Dalmiya mein kuch kala hai?' Now our judiciary demands that a plaintiff deposit 10 per cent of the amount with the court. Dalmiya withdrew his case in a hurry.

- The Satyam billboard had the funniest reaction yet. Here we're talking a major scam – Rs 7000 crores worth; Raju has been packed off to jail and the

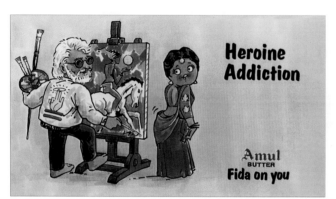

Amul's take on artist
M.F. Husain's obsession
with actress Madhuri Dixit.

company's virtually closed down. We create a hoarding where our headline screams, 'Satyam, Sharam, Scandalam!' – and we receive a typed letter from the Satyam board objecting to our billboard, demanding we apologize or else all their employees will stop using Amul products! For once, we were at a loss for words.

- Satire is a double-edged sword in India. We are a people who love to laugh. So long as the joke's not on us.

- In the good old days, spindly young men went up on rickety bamboo scaffoldings and hand-painted our hoardings, often giving our Amul girl a physique of extreme anorexia or first-level obesity, depending on their own physical orientation. There was something so romantically dangerous about a man dangling from a scaffold, trying to paint a cartoon, not because he might fall, but because there was no guarantee as to what he would reproduce.

- M.F. Husain was exactly that in his youth – a painter up on a scaffolding. He

We placed the Pakistani fast bowler on a donkey, and the headline said, 'Tab bhi phekta tha, ab bhi phekta hai!'

was thrilled with a hoarding we did on him during his Madhuri Dixit obsession. 113
It showed a cartoon of him painting the actress, and the headline said, 'Heroine Addiction'… with a sign-off – Amul: 'Fida on you'. (He asked us to gift him a small version to be placed in his studio.)

- Facebook and Twitter have become exciting options to engage the youth of India and homesick NRI audiences. Shoaib Akhtar recently made barbs at our

Sachin Tendulkar in his autobiography. We responded by placing the Pakistani fast bowler on a donkey, and the headline said, 'Tab bhi phekta tha, ab bhi phekta hai!' At last count, the FB comments were still coming in, along with 3500 'likes'.

- Nearly fifty years later, our wonderful Amul client trusts us enough to not have to show ideas to them.

Brazil's 2002 World Cup football team threw up two stars, Ronaldo and Rivaldo. We had one – 'Amul Do'.

Two of my all-time favourite hoardings.

Bombay's wonderfully designed colonial train station Victoria Terminus (VT), was renamed Chhatrapati Shivaji Terminus!

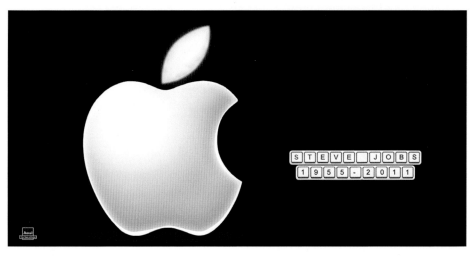

Amul mourned the death of the Apple man.

World events

The international arena has always held great fascination for the Amul hoarding – from Kuwait to Khomeini and from Osama to Obama, we've always kept our ears to the globe! Here are a few 'foren' favourites over the years…

In 1997, Hong Kong became a part of China.

In 1990, the Iraqi army invaded Kuwait.

The Libyan dictator faced the wrath of the USA, in March 2011.

An Iraqi journalist threw a shoe at President Bush, at a press meet in 2008.

Barack Obama became the first African-American president of the USA in 2008.

What 'The Wall' enjoyed when he was small

RAHUL DRAVID
Rahul Dravid is the second Indian batsman, after Sachin Tendulkar, to reach 12,000 runs in Test cricket.

The Amul campaigns were an integral part of our growing up. Waiting to see the new one on Brigade Road was one of the fun things for my brother and me while growing up in Bangalore. So to be featured on one is always nice.

The pun refers to a classic Rahul Dravid double century, as well as to his Surf detergent TV commercial, where the tag line was, 'Dho daala.'

In several Test matches, this elegant Bangalore batsman stood tall while others fell
around him.

The master batsman had many Titanic battles with South African
and Australian fast bowlers.

" Sunny bats for Amul

SUNIL GAVASKAR
Acknowledged worldwide
as one of the greatest
opening batsmen of
all time, Sunil Gavaskar
is today a well-known
and respected sports
commentator and
columnist.

The Amul hoardings are looked forward to every week
since they are so topical. It is extremely tough to pick
the best out of them since they are pretty much all-
time classics.

As for me being the subject of the hoarding,
I would hear about it from friends who would call
delightedly and describe it to me. The best
of those where I was the subject was 'Sunny, don't
let them Border you' when Allan Border's Australians
came to India.

Gavaskar had a habit of scoring double centuries.

Sunny was always the mainstay of Indian batting.

Amul is an Indian brand and it celebrates India

●●●●●

HARSHA BHOGLE

Harsha Bhogle is a popular cricket commentator, analyst and journalist. He has presented live cricket all over the world and has hosted several television programmes.

It might not have been the original intention but the now charming, now naughty, but always lovable faces on the Amul hoardings have done a fine job as chroniclers of their times. And they have done it in their own way; not with the weightiness or gravitas of a historian or with the rigour of an academic. No, that wouldn't be Amul. Instead, they have been tongue-in-cheek, have occasionally succumbed to that most journalistic of perils, the deadline, but at no stage have they stopped having fun. That is important. That is Amul.

And while not shying away from a jab at those in power, there is an unmistakable patriotism about it all. Amul is an Indian brand and it celebrates India. And like all Indians, Amul loves sport with a faintly discernible bias for cricket! And there have been some gems over the years.

But Amul the scribe has never overwhelmed Amul the brand. Amidst the wit and the topicality the brand always makes a statement. And the skill has always been in meshing the brand statement into a fun line. That is never easy and it is to the

By 1994, it was Kapil Dev's turn to set a world
record. Amul recorded it simply as 'Kapil Devours
the World.'

... the skill has always been in meshing the brand statement into a fun line.

eternal credit of those who wrote the Amul lines that the brand never lost out. As an account executive many, many years ago I was taught the importance of the brand. The Amul hoarding is fun but it is always Amul.

So let's see what the scribe said in 1983 when an Indian reached Don Bradman's record of twenty-nine Test centuries (twenty-seven years later it is a landmark that many have vaulted over but the first always remains special!). 'Don of a Sunny Era', it said simply, and charmingly played with words thereafter, 'A toast to the Little Master.'

By 1994, it was Kapil Dev's turn to set a world record. Amul recorded it simply as 'Kapil Devours the world' but by 1996, when India were crashing out of the World Cup in spite of some great batting from Sachin Tendulkar, Amul came up with a classic 'Ten du Ten don't.' And offered the kind of advice cricketers get at the boundary line in the Caribbean: 'Try some application.' It must enter Amul's Hall of Fame.

As must this one, that followed in the wake of the Harbhajan–Sreesanth slapping incident in IPL 1. Even Harbhajan, who was distraught and insecure at the time, would have permitted himself a smile. 'Pow Bhajji,' it said, and added, 'Slap it on!' Harbhajan had been on an Amul hoarding before, many years earlier, when he had spun his way into the imagination of cricket lovers in 2001 by taking 32 wickets against Australia, 'Har bhojan ke sangh.' Notice the brand is never lost!

And just to show that Amul isn't an aging brand lost in the generation of its creators came this one from IPL 3 that captured the essence of Chennai so

This must enter Amul's
Hall of Fame!

127

In the wake of the
Harbhajan–Sresanth
slapping incident in
IPL 1, Amul slapped on
this classic.

A tribute to Harbhajan
after his 32 wickets
against Australia
in 2001.

beautifully, 'Chennai Sapaad Kings. Fully yellow.' Now, not many teams in sport play in yellow and I can almost see a copywriter waiting for the moment to link the colour of Amul to a winning team!

But while it is easy to provide a chuckle when a team is winning, it isn't quite so when India lose, for I don't think we are willing to see the funny side of defeat. Yet Amul attempted it at times and it worked. After another defeat to Pakistan in the 1980s, when an unlikely hero called Manzoor Elahi emerged, Amul used Urdu to good effect, 'Wahi hota hai jo manzoore Ilahi hota hai.' But my favourite in defeat was this after India had returned from another defeat overseas, 'Hard luck boys, come home to something soft.' And then a line I loved, 'A licking you'll love!'

You would have realized that Amul has a point of view on most things, as they did about Shoaib Akhtar and his views on Sachin Tendulkar. Was Amul playing to the gallery with this classic? It doesn't matter because it captured the moment wonderfully, 'Tab bhi phekta tha, ab bhi phekta hai. Eat these words.' It showed a wonderful grasp of the language of the masses and to my mind marked another stage in its evolution.

That much for cricket. But I am going to pick two others that I absolutely adored. Along with the 2010 FIFA World Cup fever, acquiring as much of a cult status as some players was an octopus called Paul, who seemed to predict results of football matches. 'Sabka Paul khol diya! Predictably the best,' was as clever a play on words as you will see.

To show that Amul isn't an aging brand lost in the generation of its creators came this one from IPL 3 that captured the essence of Chennai so beautifully.

Seeing the funny side of defeat. Amul attempted it at times and it worked.

And, I fear I am giving away my vintage here, there was this one when India produced an unlikely win over Australia in the 1987 Davis Cup semi-final. With the rubber tied 2–2, Ramesh Krishnan, with a gentle serve and guileful ground strokes, beat the Australian Wally Masur in straight sets, and Amul said: 'Krishnan makes Masur ki daal… with Amul butter.'

Unlike paintings or other works of art that you can gaze at many times and look for layers of meaning, Amul worked on hoardings, an outdoor medium where you had a few seconds at best to create an impact. Therein lies the real genius of the Amul hoarding; around for many years but rarely, if ever, bettered.

A clever play of words about an octopus that acquired cult status at the FIFA 2010 World Cup.

The 1987 Davis Cup semi-final, when Ramanathan Krishnan defeated Wally Masur.

Timeless Amul – relevant then and now

1976

Maintain Internal Security
— Amul

With discord and disagreements between various religious, political and social factions in the country, not to mention the threat from outside, this ad is as relevant today as it was in 1976.

Electricity shortages continue in various parts
of the country thirty-three years after this ad
first appeared.

With most economists and industrialists endorsing
every budget, these ads, done in 1982–83 and 2005,
could be considered as being relevant each year!

1982

2005

The ever-increasing price of fuel!

1993

Petrol Pumped!

Amul
Affordable Fuel

The real genius of the Amul campaign

●●●●●

RAJDEEP SARDESAI

Rajdeep Sardesai is a
writer, columnist and
editor-in-chief of IBN 18
Network. He has won
several national and
international awards for
journalistic excellence.

Growing up in south Mumbai (or Bombay, as we
called it then) in the 1970s and 1980s was to live in a
wonderfully cocooned world. Traffic was manageable,
terrorism was unknown, the sea breeze was warm
and embracing, and somehow life seemed less
frenetic. So, it wasn't quite the Mumbai of a previous
Bollywood era when a Johnny Walker crooned, '*Ai dil
hai mushkil jina yahan*' on a joyful Marine Drive, but it
still was the age of innocence.

The symbols of this genteel south Mumbai were
varied: Rajabai Tower chiming away opposite the
Oval maidan, the bhelwala on Chowpatty beach,
the imposing Gateway of India dotted with pigeons,
simultaneous cricket games at the Cross and Azad
maidans, the large banyan trees along the winding
road of Walkeshwar, the leafy bylanes of Malabar Hill,
the swish set that walked down Breach Candy, the
waves lashing Marine Drive, and so much more.

There was one other durable link: the Amul
hoardings at vantage points. There was one at Pedder
Road, there was another close to the Taraporevala
aquarium along the sea face at Marine Lines. Every

The 'I love Mumbai' campaign touched a chord with all Mumbaikars.

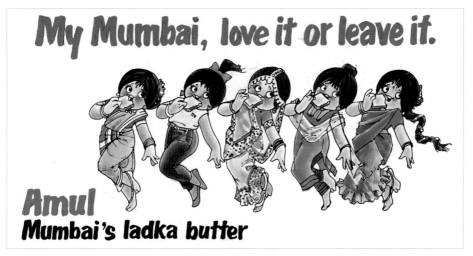

In 1995, Bombay was renamed Mumbai.

> ... there is nothing complicated in the Amul characters and their message. It is simple and accessible, identifiable to a six-year old as much as to a senior citizen.

day, our school bus would cross from one end of south Mumbai to another, a distance of just a few square kilometres, but enough for a curious group of school kids to draw in the sights and sounds of the street.

Along the road, especially as we moved from Pedder Road towards Marine Drive, there were dozens of hoardings. Mercifully, there were no large hoardings and posters greeting politicians on their birthdays at the time. Nor some tasteless, imitative Western ads. This was really the pre-liberalization era: the Indian consumer was still finding his feet, options were fewer, but there was still plenty to stare at. At nightfall, the neon light hoardings would glitter along the Queen's Necklace, each inviting you to sample their product. Amidst all the clutter, one hoarding always stood out: the Amul advertisement of the week.

What made it stand out? An easy enough question to which there is no single answer. The obvious answer would be the sheer distinctiveness of the Amul characters: others have done caricatures before and since, but somehow the ever-smiling Amul moppet captured the imagination by being refreshingly different. The difference lies perhaps in the simplicity of the execution: there is nothing complicated in the Amul characters and their message. It is simple and accessible, identifiable to a six-year-old as much as to a senior citizen.

Oh yes, there is, of course, the unique sense of humour. For most Indians, humour is associated with slapstick comedy, one reason perhaps why Mehmood became the biggest comedian on the Hindi screen. Watch any comedy show on television, and the humour is mostly loud and often rather forced. But there is

The ads have a certain irreverence for those in power, as demonstrated by this hoarding on the Ambani split.

I don't have a favourite, even though there is one on my late father that I have preserved…

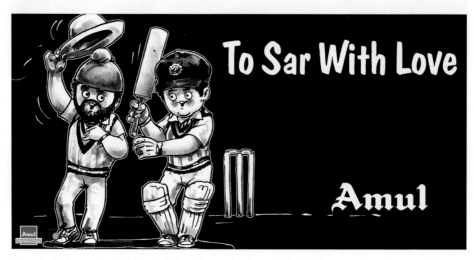

Amul bade farewell to Rajdeep's father, the ace batsman Dilip Sardesai.

nothing loud about the Amul ads. Instead, they bring alive a quality that is all too rare in Indian public life: a certain irreverence for those in power. Then, whether it is a battle between the Ambani brothers or a Congress versus BJP political war, the Amul moppet found a way to bring a smile on the face, without ever being hurtful or aggressive. Tongue firmly in cheek, the gentle wit of an Amul ad struck a chord because it was never harsh, but always contemporary.

> … the gentle wit of an Amul ad struck a chord because it was never harsh, but always contemporary.

Indeed, the real genius of the Amul campaign is that it has remained alive to the changing times. An Amitabh Bachchan may have given way to a Shah Rukh Khan, who in turn has to give way to a Ranbir Kapoor; a Sunil Gavaskar may have handed the baton to a Sachin Tendulkar, who passes it on to an M.S. Dhoni; and the political world may have moved from an Indira to a Rahul via a Rajiv, but Amul has gone on forever. Quite simply, because it has never forgotten that basic lesson of any creative endeavour: that you are only as good as your last artistic expression. So, just when you think you've seen your all-time favourite Amul ad (and frankly, I don't have a favourite, even though there is one on my late father that I have preserved), the next week will bring in another ad that will be equally utterly butterly delicious.

The closest parallel I can think of is R.K. Laxman's common man pocket cartoons in *The Times of India*. For over fifty years, Laxman has enthralled generations of Indians with his daily wit. The common man, like the Amul mascot, has become ubiquitous. What Laxman managed to do so successfully for newspaper cartoons, Amul has done for the concept of outdoor advertising: it has given it an identity, and in the process, become a chronicler of our times. Little wonder then that Amul remains the toast of the nation!

An Amitabh Bachchan may have given way to a Shah Rukh Khan, who in turn has to give way to a Ranbir Kapoor… but Amul has gone on forever.

Tickling the funny bone

●●●●●

ALYQUE PADAMSEE

Alyque Padamsee is a well-known theatre personality and is widely acknowledged as the advertising guru of India. As the head of the advertising agency Lintas, he created many outstanding and unforgettable advertising campaigns, and continues to tower over the advertising scene as a consultant.

Here, in a question and answer session conducted by Alpana Parida, this multi-talented advertising genius gives us his views on the long-standing and much-loved Amul campaign.

AP: As an eminent advertising and theatre personality, what are your impressions of the Amul advertising campaign, its format – mainly outdoor media – and how the Amul brand evolved.

ALYQUE: OK. I will just speak about all aspects of the brand and give you my views as they come to mind.

Firstly, Amul's slogan 'Utterly butterly delicious' is one of the most memorable slogans I have heard during my long advertising career. In my lifetime I have handled over 150 brands, and myself created memorable slogans and mascots for several of them, for example, Surf ('Surf ki kharidari mein samajhdari hai'), which was used for many years, and the muscle man associated with MRF tyres ('The tyre with muscle'), which is used even today. But these pale in comparison to Amul, which has a delightful tautology, the way the words are used. If it were just 'Utterly delicious,' without the 'butterly', it would not have

utterly delicious

made the impact it has today. But the phrase 'Utterly butterly delicious,' the use of these unusual words, and the way it rhymes, has given the brand its longevity. It even surpasses Nike ('Just do it'), which I think is one of the all-time-best slogans. The reason Amul is one of the most loved brands in India is because of the lovable words. And, of course, the campaign itself.

A precursor to this was the Air India campaign. My first foray into advertising was when I was working with JWT and we had to come up with topical slogans related to current happenings every week. At that time, Bobby Kooka, the marketing manager of Air India, was considered a genius in the advertising world. Air India was one of the top five airlines in the world and he was the brilliant mind behind their much-admired topical advertisements. In one of these he actually

I remember the first butter we ate in Bombay was Polson butter, and we all loved it.

used a picture of Queen Elizabeth pregnant with Prince Charles in her stomach, to introduce the jumbo jet, which I think was very irreverent. But somehow, the Air India hoardings always seemed to lack the Indian topicality that Amul had. There was always an Indian feel about the Amul topicals and that's what made them so lovable. We all like to make fun of our leaders, celebrities and situations, but usually do this only among friends. But when we see this done in public we enjoy them; something like, 'telling it like it is'. The boldness and the 'tickling the funny bone', so to say, have kept the Amul brand alive all these years.

I remember the first butter we ate in Bombay was Polson butter, and we all loved it. They had coupons on each carton, which could be collected and redeemed for gifts. But Sylvie daCunha played a brilliant stroke and came up with an idea that would require only a small budget. He was sure that hoardings would work very well and so he started off the Amul branding with just six hoardings located at prime sites. One of these was at the Chowpatty traffic light, where one invariably stopped, and it would never go unnoticed – one always wanted to wait and see what it said. Six months later, Amul became a major brand in Bombay and the Polson family quietly faded away! And since then Amul has become the most popular, and in fact, the only butter in India!

That is not to say that Amul is the best butter I have tasted. But it's the advertising that has kept the image intact. What is important is what the brand brings to the table. So, advertising and branding is like a marriage, or rather, a fusion.

Amul has to my mind without doubt done it the best. In my book, *A Double Life*, Amul plays a very important role. I have mentioned it as one of the outstanding creative icons in Indian advertising; it has been running for nearly fifty years!

So, the topicality in any advertising has to be fresh. Nana Chudasama has tried this on politics with his banner at Marine Drive, with the 'Talk of the town.'

AP: True, but the Amul moppet has dealt with various topics without any malice. So nobody ever took umbrage to what was said.

ALYQUE: Yes, the Amul girl is delightfully characterized as being cheeky, but never malicious; she is like the Barbie of India. Keeping the characterization in the cartoon or drawing style, and not bringing her into reality has made the little girl cute, sweet, naughty but never mean or evil, and that's the reason she is so loved by all.

AP: That's right; she is on the packaging. She is the brand.

ALYQUE: Yes. Yes, she is the brand ambassador for Amul.

It's like the MRF muscle man I created. It's like if you go to a tyre shop and stretch your muscles you will be offered MRF tyres. For butter, when you say 'Utterly butterly' you will be offered Amul butter. So, in a way, these become 'shop hands'. For example, if one asks, 'Kaunsa scooter chaiye?' the answer will be, 'Hamara Bajaj'.

The great thing about Amul is the agency it is associated with. Over the years daCunha has persisted with the main point. Usually, many clients tire of their

151

… she is like the Barbie of India… not bringing her into reality has made the little girl cute, sweet, naughty but never mean or evil, and that's the reason she is so loved by all.

The Onida devil has gone, the Liril girl has gone, but Amul has remained, like a pillar.

own advertising, and therefore believe that the public feels the same, and that the advertising needs to be changed. But hats off to daCunha! I can assure you that if the agency changes, the new agency is unlikely to continue with the same campaign. That's the sad part of agencies; there is a lot of competition and rivalry. For example, the Onida devil was created by the ad agency Avenues, but the day Onida switched to O&M they threw the devil out; they literally threw the brand personality out. This is also what happened to the Liril girl. They decided that the girl under the waterfall was not working for them, so they put her in the sea, the rain, then they made orange Liril, then ice cold Liril, and they finally killed the brand.

The Onida devil has gone, the Liril girl has gone, but Amul and the little girl have remained, like a pillar. These striking icons become not only the brand

memorability but the soul of the brand. This is what retains the brand loyalty. Amul
has certainly, better than anyone else, kept up to its mark.

AP: What do you think about the single medium strategy that the brand adopted?

ALYQUE: Amul's single-medium advertising strategy over the years has been remarkably brilliant. I do believe that outdoor advertising, be it kiosks, banners, or hoardings, never goes unnoticed. At some point everyone is out on the streets – whether they are walking, or in a bus or car – and if the sites are well located they will grab attention. Print and TV commercials come and go and there is a plethora of advertising – though now there are so many hoardings as well – but nevertheless hoardings create a great impact. People see them every day. Amul has never displayed its hoarding for more than two weeks. There has always been a constant change. It is something one always looks forward to. 'What is Amul going to talk about in the next ad, or what topic is Amul going to make fun of?'

I do believe that outdoor advertising, be it kiosks, banners, or hoardings, never goes unnoticed.

AP: And they have always had contemporary topics...

ALYQUE: Yes, it is always contemporary news, up-to-the-minute news! It's like your comic newspaper with the headline! And it is able to get away from too much verbiage and encapsulate just the essential part of the news and find the humour in it.

> 'Gold Finger' is my all time favourite. Forty years ago, James Bond was the rage and the movie *Goldfinger* had been released and seen by all.

The humour has been the key thing for Amul; it has always given one a chuckle. I remember forty years ago, James Bond was the rage and the movie *Goldfinger* had been released and seen by all. Amul came out with this ad, where the Amul girl is standing with her finger raised upwards with butter on it, and the caption read, 'Gold Finger.' That's the kind of memorability it has.

AP: At the time the hoardings catered mainly to the English-speaking south Bombay audiences...

ALYQUE: Yes, all the puns were in English and they appealed only to the elite. It was only later, when Bharat Dabholkar joined daCunha, that he brought in the Indian touch. The whole Hinglish thing came into existence. He introduced the local flavour. So then, fun was targeted to both: the elite class as well as

The whole Hinglish thing came into existence. Thus, the medium and the language became colloquial and appealed to a wider audience.

the common man. Thus, the medium and the language became colloquial and appealed to a wider audience.

AP: Which are the Amul ads that you find truly memorable?

ALYQUE: If I had to select one particular Amul ad, it is the 'Gold Finger' one. It is my all-time favourite. Also, 'Bitten by the love Borg' was very clever. It had a delightful pun; one had to think about it before realizing that the word 'Borg' was used instead of 'bug'! But there have been so many outstanding ones.

Amul should continue as it is... It should not change anything, otherwise it will destroy the brand.

One weak one would be, 'Roti ke neeche kya hai?' Now that it has Indianized the ads, Amul should continue as it is, and certainly not drop the hoardings and use a different medium or change the Amul girl. In fact, it should not change anything, otherwise it will destroy the brand. Coming back to Onida, the devil is now like a vague memory. It was a negative character and I had told them that this would not work, but it did. It certainly did, and I was totally wrong. The Air India maharaja worked brilliantly for the airline for so many years, until they changed it.

AP: Do you think there should be any changes to reflect the new generation?

ALYQUE: No, no, not at all. The Amul campaign reminds me of Father Christmas; he's been the same for 300 years! If you have a brand soul, you can refresh it, but never lose it.

All said and done, you simply can't separate the Amul girl and the 'Utterly butterly delicious' slogan from the Amul brand.

The Air India Maharaja
worked brilliantly for
the airline for so many
years, until they
changed it.

One weak one would
be, 'Roti ke neeche
kya hai?'

A delightful pun; one
had to think about it
before realizing that the
word 'Borg' was used
instead of 'bug'!

The power of two

●●●●●

ANIL KAPOOR
Chairman emeritus at DraftFcb Ulka, Anil has overseen the growth of the agency as one of India's top five. The agency handles Amul brands such as ice cream, milk, shrikhand and the Taste of India corporate campaign.

Great advertising is all about the power of two – a client that respects and trusts the ad agency and an ad agency that always rises to meet the needs and challenges of the client. We are fortunate to have this winning combination in Amul. An ideal client who respects the agency, daCunha Communications, and gives it a free hand, inspiring the agency to do better.

The Amul Butter campaign is the world's longest-running hoarding campaign. From welcoming Pakistan President Zia-ul-Haq with 'Pyar se Zia bhar aaye' to celebrating the election of Margaret Thatcher of the Tory party as the first woman prime minister of England with 'HistoryC choice' to encouraging Anna Hazare to break his fast with 'Kha na, Hazare,' the butter girl does it with tongue firmly in cheek.

Even after running for nearly fifty years, this is that rare campaign that everybody looks forward to eagerly week after week.

In 1986, President Zia-ul-Haq visited India.

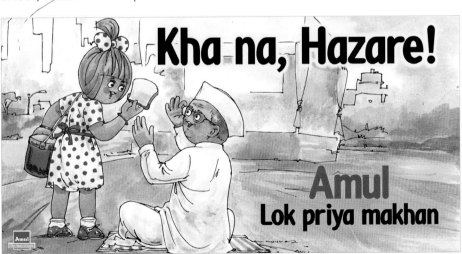

The Amul girl suggested that Anna Hazare break his fast!

The anatomy of the most loved brand in India

●●●●●

ALPANA PARIDA

Alpana Parida is president, DY Works, India's oldest and largest brand design/ brand solutions firm. DY Works has created and rejuvenated many Amul brands.

Every day, I pass by Pedder Road, looking out for the Amul hoarding for the latest in current affairs (pun intended). My all-time favourite continues to be 'Pav lo rozhi' (at the time of the 1982 World Cup, which featured Paolo Rossi), but new ones come close to it from time to time.

The unequivocal face of the brand, the Amul girl pokes fun, harasses and teases but never with any malice. She has, with her innocence, wormed her way into Indian hearts for nearly fifty years. An almost perfect personification of the Amul discourse, the campaign has become an integral part of the collective Indian consciousness. Its simple, uncomplicated style has underscored the basic Amul values of purity and innocence. The campaign has been, for the brand, a fountain of youth as its constant take on the current scenario keeps it fresh and relevant on an almost daily basis. The witty one-liners have successfully brought to fore all that vexes, amuses and/ or flummoxes us.

Though the most visible, this is but one of the many facets of the Amul brand that have helped it become one of India's most loved and trusted brands.

The Amul story is a rich tapestry of semiotic significance at many levels.

How has it achieved an almost iconic status and what is brand Amul all about? Deconstructing the brand, one finds a perfect complement between Amul the brand and the Amul girl as its brand ambassador.

The Amul story is a rich tapestry of semiotic significance at many levels. The foremost Amul discourse has to do with the nature of its business itself. Milk, ghee and butter have stood for abundance and goodness in the Indian context. Cows have been a symbol of wealth, and have been and are revered in almost all parts of

The hoarding featuring Paolo Rossi during the 1982 soccer World Cup.

Celebrating fifty years of Amul.

India since Vedic times. I grew up on stories of my grandmother's wedding where all the bulls in the groom's party (they travelled in bullock carts) were fed ghee. This was proof of her family's wealth and status as surely as the number of tolas of gold she received.

Milk and milk products have been akin to ambrosia. Being a provider of milk, therefore, is akin to divinity in the cultural context. Amul, as the primary provider of dairy products, did not have to fight any battles of acceptance. The symbolism of milk and milk products is deep. Layered on it is the extraordinarily inspiring story of the formation of a co-operative that gave livelihoods to entire villages and raised standards of living across districts, and the ensuing self-governance of a complex supply-chain-led organization that increased yields and productivity dramatically, of

Depicting the controversy raised by Menaka Gandhi about the drinking of milk.

a commitment to values before profit (even today, in the event of a milk shortage, Amul diverts its supplies to milk at much lower margins, at the cost of high-margin, value-added and processed dairy foods), and of the vision of Dr Kurien and his steering of Amul towards contributing to a White Revolution in the country.

The symbolism of milk and milk products is deep. Layered on it is the extraordinarily inspiring story of the formation of a co-operative that gave livelihoods to entire villages…

> The power of the Amul girl is that she has been distinctive and original and most of all, consistent.

Amul's witty reassurance that butter shortages were only temporary.

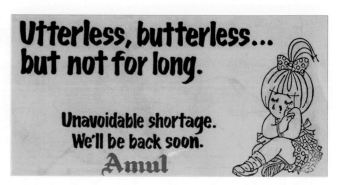

Skyscrapers became a fad in Mumbai in the 1980s.

165

Amul butter is the product that epitomizes the brand. Butter is the result of unadulterated milk and is, by nature, pure. Bal Krishna's love for butter was mythic, and is still celebrated. Krishna, as a child, has symbolized mother-child relationships. The *natkhat* Krishna has become the iconic persona that all mothers seek in their child when they say with great pride that their son is 'very naughty'.

In that context, the Amul girl is Bal Krishna!

The 'naughty' girl is immensely lovable, and all her transgressions forgiven.

This hoarding commented on the reserved quota for women in the Lok Sabha.

166

Celebrating the festival of Gokul Ashtami with a hoarding featuring the *natkhat makhanchor* Bal Krishna.

Krishna, as a child, has epitomized mother-child relationships. The *natkhat* Krishna has become the iconic persona that all mothers seek in their child when they say with great pride that their son is 'very naughty'. In that context, the Amul girl is Bal Krishna!

The illustration style is perfectly in keeping with this 'pure', childlike innocence, and the purity of the product itself. The drawing is uncluttered, not complicated, and it underscores the basic brand values. The form of humour is mostly puns that enchant with their simplicity and wit. The lines are seldom more than three or four words. All adding up to a formula that exemplifies the brand.

The power of the Amul girl is that she has been distinctive and original and most of all, consistent. She has remained mostly unchanged – and underscores another important value – consistency in quality. (There is a lesson in this consistency for large corporations with ever-changing brand managers, whose appraisals are based on what they have 'done'. Perhaps it is time to start rewarding what they have left alone.)

There is a timelessness about her that has appealed to the current generation as well. The recent Shoaib Akhtar hoarding ('Kal bhi phekta tha, aaj bhi phekta hai!') was an overnight Internet sensation and went viral very quickly.

As I drive back home tonight, I can only say: Here's looking at you, kid!

Corridors of power...

Our politicians have always been a source of inspiration and amazement for the Amul girl. The shenanigans at the centre of power, the promotion of dynastic rule, and the very personalities of our leaders, have provided us with much light-hearted amusement and entertainment.

Lampooning Lalu Prasad Yadav and Jayalalitha's misuse of power in Bihar and Tamil Nadu respectively.

Two Karnataka ministers were caught watching pornography on their phones in the legislative assembly (this topical ad resulted in 5022 'Likes' on Facebook).

When Deve Gowda became India's eleventh prime minister in 1996, Amul wondered how long his term would last!

The three Lals of Haryana politics in the 1980s – Bansi, Devi and Bhajan – battled it out for supremacy.

Sushma Swaraj of the BJP danced at Mahatma Gandhi's
samadhi in Rajghat, causing a controversy.

External Affairs Minister S.M. Krishna inadvertently read out the speech of his
Portuguese counterpart, at a UN Security Council meeting.

Blacked out!

THE PIONEER FRIDAY APRIL 26, 1996

Polls Apart!

Amul Butter: Max. Retail Price 100 g — Rs. 11.00 500 g — Rs

NOW YOU SEE IT...NOW YOU DON'T: the ad on the left was painted black by the city police be

The year 1995 was an election year (which year is not in India?!). As usual there was much infighting within the Congress party. So we ran a hoarding showing various Congress politicians in a tug-of-war over the symbol – the Hand. The Election Commission, under one T.N. Seshan, rapped us on the knuckles – he blackened out all our Amul sites – 'No political party can advertise its symbol,' was his diktat.

We were confused. We weren't a political party. But try arguing with the authorities in our country.

So we put up a rejoinder the next morning, 'If you aren't pulled up, you're pulled down.'

...d to be in violation of the electoral code of conduct. *Sudharak Olwe/Pioneer*

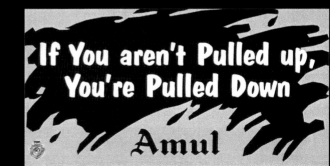
If You aren't Pulled up, You're Pulled Down

Amul

Amul has truly been involved in people's lives

●●●●●

MILIND DEORA

Son of veteran politician and MP Murli Deora, Milind is an MP from south Mumbai and minister of state for communications and information technology in the Union cabinet.

Amul is a household name that we are all familiar with. Ever since I can remember, there has been an Amul hoarding on my street in Mumbai and one has always eagerly awaited the next topic, event or personality that will be featured on it.

The Amul mascot is a lovable little girl. People tend to identify with her and so they are more tolerant of her childlike pranks and statements even on serious issues. Yet, the Amul products have also been woven into the advertisements so cleverly.

Many of the Amul products too are 'child-oriented'. For example, milk or flavoured milk, yoghurts, ice creams and, of course, the basic butter and cheese, are favourites with children.

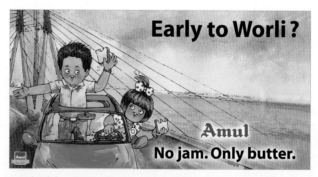

Amul celebrated the Bandra Sea Link that connects south Mumbai to the suburbs.

This hoarding referred to the abundance of young guns following in the footsteps of their politician parents.

The Amul mascot is a lovable little girl. People tend to identify with her and so they are more tolerant of her childlike pranks and statements even on serious issues.

176 Perhaps this combination of the product itself and its presentation to consumers by a playful child has contributed to making the Amul brand a household name.

As a champion of democracy, what has appealed to me is the manner in which powerful personalities, both in public and private service, have been portrayed in these hoardings. Scams, controversies and achievements have been

Milind Deora and Omar Abdullah represent the young, refreshing face of Indian politics.

Asking the reader/viewer/consumer to always vote for Amul!

depicted honestly, light-heartedly and with humour, and without
causing offence. In this way, Amul has truly been involved in the social
and cultural lives of people.

Over the years there have been so many memorable hoardings. I have
selected a few that appealed to me.

A proud moment for the country! The Indian
rupee gets a unique symbol, joins the elite
currency club.

The smart-assed little girl with the fringe...

●●●●●

SHYAM BENEGAL

Well-known film-maker
Shyam Benegal has created
and popularized a new genre
of Indian cinema and has won
several national awards for
best feature film. He has been
honoured with the Padma
Shri, the Padma Bhushan and
the Dadasaheb Phalke Award
for lifetime contribution to
Indian cinema.

My association with ASP (Advertising and Sales
Promotion Company) goes back to January 1964
when I joined the agency. Sylvester daCunha (who
headed the agency) and Usha Katrak (who handled
the Amul account), jointly created the Amul butter
campaign. There were some excellent creative people
in ASP at the time. Sylvester was always buzzing with
creative ideas, which were ably visualized by Marie
Pinto and Eustace Fernandes. It was Eustace who
visualized the smart-assed little girl with the fringe
on top. The slogan 'Utterly butterly delicious' was
Sylvester's creation.

The media strategy was to concentrate on
outdoor hoardings in towns and cities of the country.
I don't think anyone can think of Amul without
instantly recalling the Amul butter girl and the
slogan 'Utterly butterly delicious.' No other brand
has imprinted itself on the Indian mind as has that
moppet. Each week the hoardings referred to topical
news events that had caught the popular imagination.
They were invariably humorous and witty. This was
much like Air India's campaign using the mnemonic of
the maharaja, which used a similar creative strategy

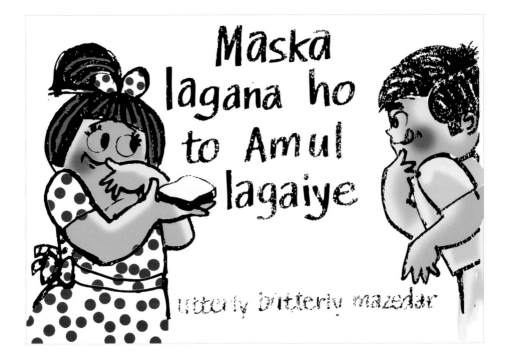

There was no television in the 1960s, and the only media available for advertising were press, outdoor, cinema and radio. For the radio, a jingle was composed using the slogan 'Utterly butterly delicious.'

180

to be in the public eye. Over the years, Air India devalued the maharaja, signalling in some ways the decline of Air India. The Amul butter girl, on the other hand, has gone from strength to strength. The moppet has endeared herself to the people of India over many generations. She appears to have become immortal, with each week relating her to some popular or even infamous event.

Amul, which has now become synonymous with all milk products in India, actually began with Amul butter, and the Amul girl was created as a rival to the village belle of Polson's butter. Today, she has become a mascot for practically all Amul products despite Amul's attempts to see her as a mnemonic for their butter.

There was no television in the 1960s, and the only media available for advertising were press, outdoor, cinema and radio. For the radio, a jingle was composed by Nathan, who was extremely popular those days. If I remember right, Nathan used to live at the foot of Malabar Hill, which was very wooded at the time, and had a whole menagerie of animals and birds running free in his home. He reminded one of St Francis while he sat and composed music on his harmonium. There would be a myna or a parrot perched on his shoulder or even on his balding head, with squirrels running up and down the rafters and monkeys eating peanuts on the verandah. The jingle he composed was used both for radio as well as for film commercials for a long time. A few years later, my daughter Pia, who had just started her kindergarten, gave her voice for the line 'Utterly butterly delicious,' which eventually became the signature of all radio and film advertising.

When I gave up advertising to become an independent film-maker, I was often called upon to make film commercials for Amul. Amul baby food had just

Today, she has become a mascot for practically all
Amul products despite Amul's attempts to see her
as a mnemonic for their butter.

come into the market then, and much like outdoor hoardings that were primarily used for butter, baby food was advertised using film commercials. This was a time when people believed that only cow's milk was fit for baby food. Amul baby food was different. It was made from buffalo milk. It had to fight consumer prejudice and if that was not bad enough, had to contend with multinationals that controlled the baby food market at the time. The man who changed the equation was Dr V. Kurien. Dr Kurien was and is an extraordinary figure in the milk co-operative movement. He led the way to make India the largest milk-producing nation in the world, a feat achieved in a span of no more than twenty-five years. When Amul started the first milk co-operative in Anand, India was not even producing enough milk to meet the nation's requirement. Making and marketing baby food from buffalo milk was his innovation. In a short time, the various myths and prejudices regarding buffalo milk disappeared and soon enough Amul baby food became the largest and the most popular baby food in the country.

The year 1965 was a very difficult one for India. We had barely recovered from the India-China War of 1962, when we were locked in armed conflict with Pakistan. Our resources were being drained and famine loomed large on the horizon. For Prime Minister Lal Bahadur Shastri, raising agricultural production in India became the top priority. He coined the now-famous slogan, 'Jai Jawan, Jai Kisan,' at the time. One hugely successful programme then was the milk co-operative movement in Gujarat, under the leadership of Dr Kurien. Shastri visited Anand and studied the farmers' co-operatives there and even travelled incognito

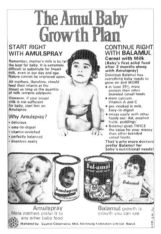

Amul baby food advertising from the 1960s.

Much like outdoor hoardings that were primarily
used for butter, baby food was advertised using
film commercials.

> I realized that there were many human interest stories that could make a feature film that could be both entertaining and persuasive.

at night to meet farmers in their own homes without the knowledge of his security detail, helped in this endeavour by Dr Kurien. It took some time for farmers to recognize the prime minister. It was a huge event for both the prime minister and Dr Kurien. While the PM got unvarnished first-hand experience and understanding of how the co-operatives worked, Dr Kurien had an extremely restless night. When he rushed the next morning to meet the prime minister, he found a beaming Shastri having already made up his mind as to what he would like to do. He wanted to replicate Amul's success in all other parts of India. This signalled the birth of the National Dairy Development Board (NDDB), and on Dr Kurien's insistence, it had its head office in Anand, which was home to Amul. Not only did NDDB have its headquarters in the heart of rural India but an Institute of Rural Management also came up on its campus. All of this led rapidly to the enormous growth of the milk co-operative movement in the country, making India the largest milk producer in the world.

The birth of NDDB triggered the milk revolution in the country. An ambitious programme called Operation Flood was launched by Dr Kurien to help accelerate milk production in the country by creating milk co-operatives in all the milksheds in the country. Another strategy followed by the NDDB under Dr Kurien was to create spearhead groups that travelled from village to village to convince farmers of the benefits of creating milk co-operatives, both to maximize their profits from milk and also to help improve the quality of their livestock.

In all, I produced two documentary films on the two phases of Operation Flood. During the course of research and shooting of these documentaries, I

realized that there were many human interest stories that could make a feature film that could be both entertaining and persuasive. The documentaries I had made were more for an audience consisting of World Bank officials, the World Health Organization, the United Nations and officials of the Government of India. The films could only be shown to people at special screenings. Given the situation with documentaries, the films would only be preaching to the converted. Mapping the stories of the farmers would be much more persuasive and entertaining to general audiences.

Dr Kurien did not need too much convincing. In fact, he came up with a novel way of raising money to make the film, by getting the farmers themselves

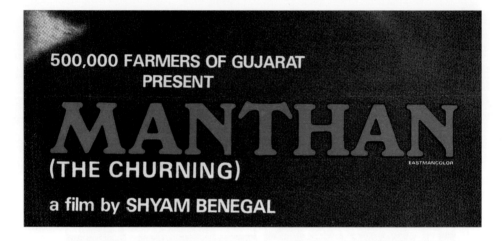

The contribution that each farmer member of the co-operative had to make could not have been more than a couple of rupees. It helped raise a million rupees to produce the film *Manthan* (The Churning).

The film turned out to be a huge success with cinema audiences and with farming and rural communities.

to produce the film. I had made up my mind that my film production company and I would take no professional fees. This helped in bringing the cost down. The contribution that each farmer member of the co-operative had to make could not have been more than a couple of rupees. It helped raise a million rupees to produce the film *Manthan* (The Churning).

The film turned out to be a huge success with cinema audiences and also with farming and rural communities. It was exciting to see truckloads of milk farmers coming from the villages and districts of Gujarat to its cities to see what was arguably a film that they had produced. Nothing could have been more satisfying for a film maker like myself than to see a film succeed where it mattered most.

188

GUJARAT CO-OPERATIVE MILK MARKETING FEDERATION LTD.

500,000 FARMERS OF GUJARAT
PRESENT

MANTHAN
EASTMANCOLOR

(THE CHURNING)

a film by **SHYAM BENEGAL**

Featuring
**GIRISH KARNAD • SMITA PATIL • NASEERUDDIN SHAH
ANANT NAG • AMRISH PURI • KULBHUSHAN • MOHAN AGASHE
SADHU MEHER**

PHOTOGRAPHY:	SCREENPLAY:	DIALOGUE:	MUSIC:
GOVIND NIHALANI	VIJAY TENDULKAR	KAIFI AZMI	VANRAJ BHATIA
EDITING:	PRODUCTION CONTROL:	PROCESSED AT:	
BHANUDAS DIWKAR	G. B. GHANEKAR	BOMBAY FILM LAB PVT. LTD.	

GIRISH KARNAD   SMITA PATIL

AMRISH PURI   KULBHUSHAN

MANTHAN relates the story of a young urban group headed by a veterinary doctor, which is sent by an organisation to a poor village in order to help start a milk cooperative.

As they proceed, they come up against two kinds of vested interests. One, a private contractor who has been exploiting the village for years and two, the village headman who sees in the cooperative a means to strengthen his own power.

The team leader, who can see this thinks that if he could get the poor majority (who also happen to belong to the harijan community—or the out-castes) into the cooperative, he can thwart the headman.

This is not as easy as he imagines. He picks a natural leader from among them, Bhola. Bhola is initially against this outside intrusion in his village. He suspects all outsiders and sees them only as exploiters. He has good reason. His own father, an urban contractor, abandoned his mother. And one of the members of the group is already carrying on with a village girl. Gradually, he comes to see the value of the cooperative.

In the process, however, the dormant caste antagonisms are brought to the surface and cause a clash. This results in the burning of the harijans' huts. The private contractor sees this opportunity to get back his influence with the villagers. Everything appears to have reverted to the way it always was. The village goes back to the old ways. The team now in despair, is asked by the organisation to leave the village.

There is one ray of hope. Bhola. He has seen what the cooperative means for a village.

NASEERUDDIN SHAH   ANANT NAG

MOHAN AGASHE   SADHU MEHER

मंथन की कहानी शहरी नौजवानों के एक दल की कहानी है जो दूध उत्पादकों की सहकारी समिति बनाने की योजना लेकर एक पिछड़े गाँव में जाते हैं। एक संस्था द्वारा प्रेषित इस दल का नेता एक पशु चिकित्सक है।

Apart from its commercial run, the film has been used by spearhead teams of the NDDB for almost two-and-a-half decades to persuade and encourage milk farmers to create milk co-operatives all over the country.

A tribute to Dr Kurien on his 90th birthday.

It has been my privilege to have known and worked with Dr Kurien.

The film itself has had an exciting history. Apart from its commercial run it has been used by spearhead teams of the NDDB for almost two-and-a-half decades to persuade and encourage milk farmers to create milk co-operatives all over the country. Later, it was also used by the United Nation's Development Programme (UNDP) to promote the creation of milk co-operatives in various countries of South Africa, Latin America and Asia. When Morarji Desai was prime minister, he gave prints of the film as gifts to the governments of China and the Soviet Union. I am told that the Institute of Rural Management, Anand, uses *Manthan* in its courses even today, thirty-five years later. The credit for all of this clearly goes to Dr Kurien.

In 1997, I produced a ten-part television series called *Sankranti* to commemorate fifty years of Indian independence. Two episodes were dedicated to each decade, highlighting the events and evolution of India's polity; political and social developments, and economic growth during the first fifty years of independent India. The decade of the 1960s was devoted to the Green Revolution that was ushered in Punjab by Dr M.S. Swaminathan and the White Revolution ushered in by Dr Kurien. For me, the greatest heroes of Indian independence of the last half a century are these two, along with Homi Bhabha and Vikram Sarabhai. They are the true heroes of our country. It has been my privilege to have known and worked with Dr Kurien.

So what goes into an Amul ad?

●●●●●

MANISH JHAVERI

An award-winning copywriter, Manish Jhaveri counts the Marx Brothers, Monty Python and Woody Allen as his sources of inspiration. Manish has been writing the Amul hoardings since 1994. He is a creative consultant to a slew of agencies and also regularly scripts international events, awards shows and websites.

The poem covers my stint at Amul, the way we go about creating an ad, some of our favourite topics, and a bit on the way Amul has influenced the language people use.

Utterly butterly delirious

I'm younger than the Amul campaign,
But the moppet shines like an old flame;
Having drooled over Amul since school,
Doing these lines now is truly cool!

In '94 my dream came true;
I unwrapped my first line my debut!
The Maska Mascot smiled by my side,
Go on, she said, spread this smile far and wide!

News became a ruse to get one amused,
From Ten du Ten don't, to Buttered and Bruised;
Bhooth became Bhookh; Bill Cleaned Town,
Iwannasandwich with Goran's crown!

So what goes into an Amul ad?
Deadlines are crazy; headlines, mad!

News became a ruse to get one amused.

193

Film-maker Ram Gopal Verma's horror film, *Bhoot*, was the inspiration for this 2003 hoarding.

President Clinton's visit to Mumbai in 2000, 'motivated' the Bombay Municipal Corporation to clean up the city.

Croat Goran Ivanisevic won his only Wimbledon crown in 2001 as a wildcard.

Cricket fits Amul to a tea,
When Sachin's in form, so are we!

The Little Master's appetite for runs is insatiable.

In 1998, Sir Don Bradman compared his own batting style to that of Tendulkar's.

One cannot slip, one cannot let up;
Ideas spring the moment one gets up.

Always pressure to keep things fresher,
Last line was fine; this better be better!

A typical topical shapes up,
With a telephonic gup-shup:
Wanna roast that chump or toast this champ?
So much to say, our lips can't be clamped!

One cannot slip, one cannot let up;
Ideas spring the moment one gets up;
Scan the front page; what's the set up?
Feed your wit but don't get fed up!

These are a few of our favourite things,
Hoardings starring Bollywood bling,
Right on top sits Mr Bachchan,
He's a real hero for our makhan!

Then there's our playing eleven!
Now that's a match made in heaven!
Cricket fits Amul to a tea,
When Sachin's in form, so are we!

196   And politics gives us our kicks,

There's so much to pick, so much to lick!

It's Delhi's dirty underbelly,

All's fair in this mela and melee!

To us controversy is not new,

We raise issues; sometimes, hackles too!

There are many who can't take a joke,

They find it hard to like our poke!

Amul's influence is hard to miss;

Newspaper headlines reflect this!

Packed with puns, and tons of Hinglish,

There's a dash of Amul in every dish!

Once you start, you just can't stop it,

For job fulfilment, you can't top it;

Amul's good as gold and just as precious,

Utterly butterly delicious!

Packed with puns, and tons of Hinglish,
There's a dash of Amul in every dish!

On winning the 2011 World Cup.

On the cult classic song, 'Kolaveri Di'.

The complex process of creativity

A RECORD OF THE AMUL HOARDINGS WAS PREVIOUSLY MAINTAINED IN A SERIES OF 'GUARD BOOKS' INTO WHICH THE ORIGINAL SKETCHES WERE PASTED. TODAY, A DIGITAL RECORD OF THE HOARDINGS IS RETAINED INSTEAD.

ARTIST JAYANT RANE'S
SKETCHES SEEM
TO EFFORTLESSLY CAPTURE
THE ESSENCE OF THEIR
SUBJECT MATTER BUT
ARE THE RESULT OF
PAINSTAKING REFINEMENT.

ONCE A SKETCH IS FINISHED IT IS HAND-COLOURED.

Step-by-step

Once upon a time, every hoarding was hand-painted.

Now technology has evolved – and glitzy vinyls are draped on the Amul hoardings.

AND TO THE
HOARDING SITES
EVERY FRIDAY

THE ARTWORK IS
DELIVERED DIGITALLY

120 HOARDINGS
WERE PRODUCED
IN 2011 – ONE
EVERY THREE
DAYS!

A NEW
HOARDING MUST
BE DELIVERED
TO THE MEDIA EVERY
TUESDAY

THE SKETCHES
ARE REFINED AND
HAND-COLOURED

DEADLINES ARE
TIGHT

THE SUBJECT OF
THE HOARDING IS
DECIDED

THE ARTIST PREPARES
INITIAL SKETCHES

From concept to hoarding

THE AMUL GIRL HOLDING A MAP SHOWING THE LOCATION OF THE 90 AMUL HOARDINGS IN INDIA.

AMUL TOPICALS ARE ALSO SIMULTANEOUSLY PRINTED IN 22 NEWSPAPERS ACROSS THE COUNTRY, SHOWN ON TV CHANNELS, ON AMUL.COM, AND 'LIKED' ON WWW.FACEBOOK.COM/ AMUL.COOP.

The life of the dead placed in the memory of the living...

1988

The great showman, Raj Kapoor, smiled his last.

1992

DIRECTOR

Satyajit Ray
1921-Forever

Amul

He lived his life in 35mm.

Avjo, JRD

Amul

We said Tata to the great man.

1994

AMAR, AKBAR, ANTHONY
& AMUL
BID YOU FAREWELL, MAN*ji*.

We lost the 'lost-and-found formula' man, Manmohan Desai.

1994

He was the founder chairman of Amul.

1997

The wonderful Princess Diana died tragically.

She was truly everyone's mother.

1998

Mona Darling and all of us bade Bollywood villain Ajit goodbye.

2001

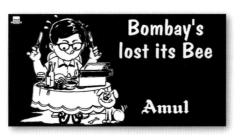

The city lost its funny bone when Behram Contractor passed on.

Dadamoni RIP.

The quiet Beatle went silent.

2003

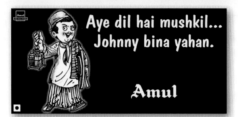

Johnny Walker walked into the sunset with a smile.

2004

Mehmood will always be the original comic.

He was Amul's tech wizard.

The Bollywood baddie Amrish Puri was one of life's good guys.

2005

Sunil Dutt was an actor and politician par excellence.

2009

His life was a true thriller.

2011

He was the artist of all painters.

Amul's tribute to a slain journalist.

■ The new Amul Butter hoarding is a final tribute to Busybee, the Father of Foodies in Bombay, and the pioneer of the eating out column. "Bombay has lost its Bee," says the hoarding, "and so have we at daCunhas," wrote the advertising geniuses behind the Amul campaign, Rahul, Nisha and Sylvie daCunha.

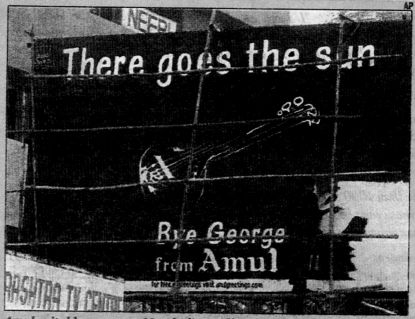

Amul suitably expresses Mumbai's goodbye to Beatle George Harrison who died of throat cancer on November 29. Bye, bye love

M.A.K. Pataudi: cricketer and gentleman.

He danced and rocked his way into our hearts.

Pandit Bhimsen Joshi was the singer of singers.

Dev Anand was evergreen and everloved.

The great cartoonist led an illustrious life.

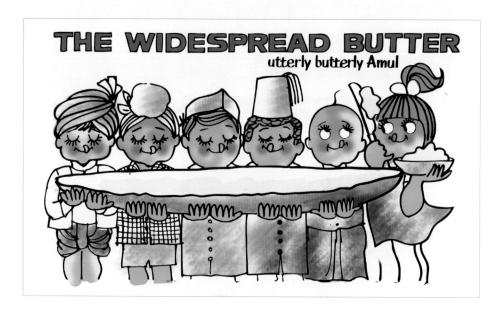